**Also by the authors**

*Healing Addictions: The Vulnerability Model of Recovery*
*Dante's Path: A Practical Approach*
*to Achieving Inner Wisdom*
*Dante's Path: Vulnerability and the*
*Spiritual Journey (2nd ed.)*
*Florentine Promise: A Seeker's Guide*
*Transpersonal Development: Cultivating the Human*
*Resources of Peace, Wisdom, Purpose and Oneness*

Praise for **The End of Fear**

The Schaubs have written a masterpiece for reducing fear and finding balance in one's life— one of the most elegant, clearest, and effective treatises available."

– Larry Dossey, MD, author of *One Mind: How Our Individual Mind Is Part of Greater Consciousness and Why It Matters*

The Schaubs' significant contributions to understanding vulnerability could not come at a better time for a world struggling to find a way through profound suffering. They offer a way to transform our relationship with our own vulnerability into a healing connection with our inner resources for peace. *The End of Fear* to anyone seeking a deeper experience with *life as it is* in order to thrive in even the most difficult of times.

– Heidi Taylor, PhD, RN

*The End of Fear* makes a dramatic promise and fulfills that promise in every story, suggestion or ancient wisdom offering. How do we cope with life's inevitable vulnerabilities, including death?
Bonney and Richard, with decades of clinical experience share their own vulnerability stories while offering a path to transform our deepest fears into a realistic stance on how we can face life and live it fully, moment to moment. In my practice, when a patient is struggling with life's inevitable losses, I recommend that they read this book.

– Barry Simon, MD, psychiatrist, psychoanalyst

According to a well known Talmudic saying, "Words that come from the heart enter the heart."
This book will speak to you personally and guide you to accept and transform your own vulnerability into strength and wisdom.

– Dr. Yoav Datillo, Past president of the Italian Association for Psychosynthesis Psychotherapy (SIPT) and past vice president of the European Association for Psychosynthesis Psychotherapy (EFPP)

# The End of Fear

*Vulnerability as a Spiritual
Path for Realists*

BONNEY SCHAUB
*and*
RICHARD SCHAUB

Archway Publishing books may be ordered
through booksellers or by contacting:

Archway Publishing
1663 Liberty Drive
Bloomington, IN 47403
www.archwaypublishing.com
844-669-3957

Interior Image Credit: Ava Grace Brosnan

ISBN: 978-1-6657-2499-9 (sc)
ISBN: 978-1-6657-2500-2 (e)

Library of Congress Control Number: 2022910896

Print information available on the last page.

Archway Publishing rev. date: 8/31/2022

With gratitude to
Massimo Rosselli and Richard Grossman

# Contents

# Author's Note

I have written this book in the first person in order to openly show my own fears and vulnerabilities, but everything in it is also the work of my wife, Bonney Gulino Schaub. All the insights and practices here have been tested, retested, and refined in our work and in our relationship.

The people, events, and dialogues presented in this book are taken from our 40 years of practice as psychotherapists and Clinical Meditation and Imagery (CMI) teachers. All identifying details have been changed to protect the privacy of the individuals.

# Preface to the 2<sup>nd</sup> Edition

*In all nations there are minds which incline
to dwell in the conception of the fundamental
Unity.*

—Ralph Waldo Emerson

Sometime after the publication of the first edition (2009) of
*The End of Fear: A Spiritual Path for Realists,* we were invited
to train health professionals in Florence, Italy. During the
second day of training, an exasperated doctor said that she
had been waiting and waiting for us to present the answer –
how to get rid of vulnerability. When we replied that you
can't get rid of it, but you can learn how to live with full
acceptance of it and receive the benefits of that acceptance,
the doctor shrugged, showing her displeasure with this
response.

We are not making fun of this physician. She was a
perfectly rational person who simply wanted a reasonable
answer for getting rid of the number one emotional challenge

in the entire human world – awareness of our vulnerability and the fear and anxiety it provokes in us. In *The End of Fear,* we wanted to state the problem as plainly and directly as possible and utilize this undeniable fact as an inner path to finding peace. Letters from around the world told us that we had partially articulated the path in the book, but others were like the good Florentine doctor who was displeased that we offered no escape route.

In fact, we have found two answers in our vulnerability. The first is full acceptance of it by realizing that every living being in the entire world, including us, is vulnerable and that we are all in this together: as Dante expressed it, "*We are all in our little boats out on the great ocean of being.*"

There can be compassion and solace in the fact that we are not alone, that absolutely everyone you see, without exception, is in exactly the same boat as you are. No special status, no great beauty, no wealth, no scientifically-backed special diet, no fame grants you an exception from this factual reality of being vulnerable in this world.

The second answer in our vulnerability is utilizing it as a motivator to open up to seeking and discovering more about reality. If we start out with the fact that reality includes the mystery of death, what other mysteries exist that we don't yet know about? This second answer has been the basis of the spiritual search worldwide and throughout time – to seek and experience non-visible realities that help us reconcile with our vulnerability.

An earlier book of ours, *Dante's Path: Vulnerability and the Spiritual Journey,* and two books after *The End of Fear - The Florentine Promise* and *Transpersonal Development* – described the discoveries of seekers and, in some cases, their life-changing impact. Perhaps the single unifying theme of such discoveries is a state of *oneness* in which the separate, frightened self drops away and is replaced by the quiet joy and bliss of connection and participation in something greater than ourselves. *Something more.*

As we write this, there is a trend in medicine to introduce psychedelic drugs into healthcare so that people in life-challenging physical and mental health crises can possibly experience discoveries about non-visible realities and receive the peace of knowing that there is *something more* than this body and this mind. Based on our over 40 years of clinical experience with hundreds of patients and clients, we know that people can experience these same results without psychedelics. In fact, such transpersonal discoveries have become the major focus of our work.

*The End of Fear* lays the groundwork for this seeking through the stories of people of all ages, ill and healthy, who feel the need and the longing to know *something more.* We wrote it, as Emerson said, for those "who incline to dwell… in the fundamental Unity."

# Introduction

## *The 3 a.m. Mind*

*My humanity is bound up in yours, for we can
only be human together.*

— Desmond Tutu

It was three o'clock in the morning in a small hotel room in
Paris, and I was wide-awake. We were supposed to fly home
the next afternoon, but my wife, Bonney, had a severe and
painful ear infection, and in the next room I could hear our
pregnant daughter retching from her morning sickness. In
my 3 A.M. mind, I imagined we would miss our flight and
be stuck here, in these two small rooms in a foreign country,
until our money ran out. Then it occurred to me that the
unusual ache in my head, which I'd had off and on since
the day before, was a brain tumor. It was a remarkably clear
and convincing thought.

    I tried to go back to sleep, but some bad door in my

mind had swung open and more fears came crowding in. I saw images of dead children crushed under bombed buildings, their frantic parents digging like animals to get to the bodies. I saw women in head scarves cover their faces and sob. I remembered that the ache in my head really was a tumor—that it wasn't just my mind playing tricks on me—and then I told myself that couldn't be true, and then I realized that it was. I imagined myself disoriented, collapsing, lying unconscious on a street in Paris while my wife and daughter begged for money in a corner of the Gare de Lyon train station.

On and on it went, a total takeover. I saw a flood of apocalyptic images—starvation, killing, anarchy. I recognized the world as a place of war, stupidity, and greed that would inevitably destroy all the goodness in life. I saw that all my relationships were fake, all of us performing in masks and pretending to care. I got angry at my mind for torturing me with these thoughts, but it immediately countered by throwing The Big One back at me: "You're having these thoughts because you've gone insane." I lay back on the bed, stared at the ceiling, and begged the God I no longer believed in to stop my mental breakdown.

What really happened, after all this drama and torment? Nothing except a crazed, sleepless night. The next morning Bonney and I went to the American Hospital and consulted with a wonderful physician. Medication was prescribed and we were told it was okay for her to fly. My daughter felt a little better, and we flew home as scheduled. Even if we hadn't, we would have figured something out. After all, I was over 60 years old and had a lot of life experience; how hard would it have been to get by in the great city of Paris for a little while? In the light of day, I knew this reasonable view to be true. But in my 3 A.M. mind, the only true thing was my fear.

Sitting in the plane waiting to take off for New York, I savored the normality of people talking to one another, the announcement of the funny in-flight movie, the courtesy of the flight crew. I felt safe and secure. I had my experience in the hotel room in perspective; I believed that what I had gone through was a purging of accumulated fear in my system. I figured I'd gotten it *out* of my system, at least for a while.

My perspective didn't last long. Three days later, I was driving into Manhattan to go back to work. For those of you who don't know New York, there's a tunnel between Long Island and Manhattan that goes under the East River. Just before you enter the tunnel, you can see the whole New York skyline—all the way from the Empire State Building and the United Nations north to the 59th Street and Bronx-Whitestone Bridges, and, looking south, the empty space on the horizon where the twin towers of the World Trade Center used to be. The road that feeds into the tunnel, the Long Island Expressway, is considered to be one of the busiest highways in the world, so traffic jams and backups are the norm.

On this particular morning, the traffic was barely moving. Glancing around at the other drivers, I saw one young man reading a thick textbook propped up on his steering wheel: I guessed that he was certain we were in for a long wait. Eventually our snarl of cars crawled and merged into two lanes and we entered the tunnel. Then about midway through we came to a dead halt, the brake lights of hundreds of cars and trucks lighting up the tunnel walls in red.

After a few minutes, with no signs of moving and the noxious smells of heavy exhaust seeping into my car, I felt a jump in my nerves, a big shift toward anxiety. I had the impulse to open all the windows, but I knew that would only make me feel worse.

And then I heard a dull boom from somewhere up ahead, farther up the tunnel. I imagined that a bomb had gone off, breaching the tunnel walls and exposing us all, trapped in our cars, to the full force of the river bursting through. In my imagination, I frantically looked in both directions to decide which end of the tunnel to swim for. As the water rose toward the tunnel roof, I realized I'd have to swim out underwater. Down in the pit of my stomach, I knew I wouldn't make it out of the tunnel alive.

I saw my drowned body bobbing up to the surface of the river and floating downstream on currents made swift and choppy by the bomb blast. I saw a passerby on the riverbank watching the hundreds of other bodies, body parts, car parts, and tunnel parts all flowing toward the Statue of Liberty and then out into the Atlantic. Did that person on the riverbank see dead me? Was he noting my passing as I drifted out to my final resting place under the waves?

Then the line of red brake lights in front of me went out, the traffic started up, and I snapped out of my drowning and back into the present moment, moving forward again.

## The Roots of Fear

> *Nothing in life is to be feared it is only to be understood. Now is the time to understand more, so we may fear less.*
>
> — Marie Curie

As psychotherapists and meditation teachers, Bonney and I have made a career of examining the mind's intriguing activities. Drawing upon the healing principles of many spiritual and psychological traditions, from Zen and mindfulness and Qi Gong meditation and Christian and Sufi mysticism to biofeedback, insight-oriented psychotherapy, imagery, and the transpersonal psychology of psychosynthesis, we've had 40 years of experience helping to solve the intimate inner struggles of hundreds of people, including fears just like mine and probably just like yours, too.

During the course of a normal day, your fears probably show themselves in much milder, manageable forms. You become absorbed in worry for a few minutes; you replay over and over a critical comment someone made to you; you get nervous about something new you have to do; you feel the rising of anger in reaction to someone who seems to dislike you. Chances are you don't envision Armageddon or your own catastrophic end on a daily basis. Still, our common human sensitivity to feeling vulnerable, to becoming nervous or afraid, is probably affecting you, causing tension in your neck, back, or stomach and stirring up anxious anticipation of future events that may never come to pass. While my breakdown in Paris and my drowning in the tunnel may be dramatic examples, the truth is that our minds spend as much time wrestling with the many forms of fear and imagined threats to survival as they do connecting in a loving way to life.

This book has been written with the desire to relieve that fear.

To do this, I need to tell you about a curious discovery that dawned on us at some point during Bonney's and my decades of professional practice. From privileged heiresses and movie idols to lost souls on their second psychiatric hospitalization or their third stay in rehab, we were hearing the same story again and again: the story of the fear that rose up in them when they fully recognized—whether because of a great disappointment, a separation, an illness, a death, or simply their own spiritual questioning—that life is unpredictable and fragile and guarantees loss. Catholic priests and nuns, Jewish rabbis, Protestant ministers, and Muslim imams all consulted with us to get help with their own fears and to replenish themselves for the work of helping others—for consoling the next parent of a baby born handicapped or the next family that lost a loved one in a senseless accident.

We explored these people's fears with focused attention, and this is what we found: When you follow fear down to its deepest roots, you always come out on the other side in a field of love. Simply put, we discovered that the origin of fear is the love of life. This book is a spiritual journey to help you make this discovery for yourself and to experience its benefits in your life—to bring an end to fear as you know it.

We won't do this by trying to convince you that your fear is irrational or unfounded or something to be suppressed or denied. That's just the point: Your fear isn't irrational—it is *real*. On the realistic spiritual path that you'll be learning about in this book, fear is treated as a fact that can be appreciated, understood, and transformed. Until you know the way to transform fear, it will erode your confidence and diminish your experience of life at every turn by arousing its companion feelings of anxiety or anger in your mind and tension or contraction in your body. Once you know the way to transform it, you'll be freed to realize more and more fully your potential for joy, oneness, and love—the innate spiritual qualities that you brought with you when you came into this world and that reside, dormant, in you right now.

## The Realistic Path

> *I believe that we must find, all of us together,*
> *a new spirituality.*
>
> — The Dalai Lama

The first stage of the journey is cultivating a new view of the people around you: Everyone you see, without exception, is vulnerable.

What do we mean by "vulnerable"? The root of the word is the Latin *vulnus,* "wound," so literally it means something like "susceptible to wounding." Vulnerability shows up as a feeling, yes—a feeling of nervousness and insecurity that comes of being susceptible to wounding, exposed to risk— but it is more than a feeling. It is the state we all live in; it is our actual human situation. No matter how we try to deny it, we know deep down that life is unpredictable and that we risk change and loss at every moment. And no matter how tough other people look on the outside, on the inside they're just as vulnerable as you; even the strongest man on Earth lives in a state of utter fragility. No special religion grants any of us an exemption, and no amount of money or status can change this core fact of life. Our vulnerability lies in the transitory nature of our lives, and we're all in this together.

There's nothing new about this view in itself. Buddhists know the truth we've just described; they call it "the truth of impermanence." Philosophers of both East and West know it as "the human condition." Modern psychology has grasped it, too, describing the fight/flight instinct in each of us that arises when the underlying fear we live with is triggered.

We'll show you, through specific, intimate examples, the three classic choices people make to cope with their vulnerability. Some embed themselves in materialism, others pin their hopes on religion, and still others step back from life to take refuge in disengaged skepticism. Through their stories, you'll see that each of these types is trying to turn away from fear—but our discovery is that something of fundamental emotional and spiritual importance only begins to happen when you turn around and face it.

The second stage of the journey is training yourself in how to *skillfully* turn toward your fear. Since your vulnerability isn't going to go away, the wisest thing you can do is to learn to be with it, and we'll show you how.

We'll explain the reasons behind the training, and we'll show you what, in our experience, works and doesn't work. We'll be training you to practice *the awareness of vulnerability* while you're around other people, out in nature, or just thinking your own private thoughts. We'll lay the foundation for a kind of constant, instant practice that you can do anytime, anywhere.

As you begin to practice, the third stage of the journey appears on its own. You might say it comes to meet *you* rather than the other way around. The more you accept your vulnerability and take gentle care of your fear, the more you will feel connected to every other living being—and the more you will feel your deep, innate love toward all living beings, including yourself.

This connecting love, this all-encompassing and uplifting sense of oneness, is your innate spiritual potential. It rises up because it was always there, in the ground of your being, only held down by fear. We'll show you how it has arisen in the lives of people we've worked with, and how it's changed their lives. We'll help you grasp that it can happen for you, too, and that the title of this book can become the way you walk around in the world.

# PART I

## understanding fear

*The need for real answers has grown exponentially
with the awareness of the real problems we
are facing in our social, political, health and
environmental worlds. This search is especially
active and even urgent in our adolescents
and young adults who can view life globally
more than any generation before them.*

# 1

## The Human Condition

*I remembered that the real world was wide,*
*and that a varied field of hopes and fears, of*
*sensations and excitements, awaited those who*
*had the courage to go forth into its expanse,*
*to seek real knowledge of life amidst its perils.*
— Charlotte Bronte

Though she had an important meeting the next morning, Anne couldn't fall asleep. She pleaded with herself to relax so she could go into the meeting calm and well rested, but sleep would not come. She looked at the clock's glowing red numbers: 1:30 A.M., 2:00, 2:30. She began to feel panicky and told herself not to look at the clock again, but then she did: 2:45. She tossed and turned, got up, went to the bathroom, got back into bed, tossed and turned, telling herself, *Don't look at the clock.* At some point she must have dropped off, for the next thing she knew, the alarm was going off, waking her at 7.

When Anne had finished telling me her story, I asked her, "How did the meeting go?" Fine, she said, although she was a nervous wreck and was glad when it ended.

What was the fear that had kept her up all night?

She was worried that she might have to speak at the meeting.

What was scary about that? Hadn't she spoken at many meetings before this?

Yes, of course; she had been in the business for ten years and had spoken at countless meetings. But each time it was torture anticipating the moment when she'd have to speak up.

What was the fear?

Anne thought for a moment, then said, "I might look nervous."

And what would happen then?

She answered at once: "I'd look like I don't know what I'm talking about."

Even though she'd been successful in her job for ten years?

"Yes—I'd look bad."

And then?

Anne paused, her face beginning to reflect a deeper

concern. "They wouldn't want me," she said. "They'd replace me."

And what would happen *then?*

One by one, we peeled back the layers of Anne's fear. Her firm would start to see other workers as more valuable. Anne would be demoted. Then she would be fired. Without a good recommendation from her employer, she wouldn't be able to find another job. She would run out of money, she would lose her apartment, and she would end up on the street.

Suddenly we'd arrived at Anne's version of my Paris nightmare—my vision of myself collapsing, destitute and broken, on the sidewalk outside the Gare de Lyon. That fear had come over me in the small hours, too—the time of night when little children wake in terror of the monster in the closet and seek the safety of their parents' bed. As adults, we're supposed to know that the monster is make-believe, but in fact it's as real as our own anxieties; it simply takes a different form.

What is the source of this fear inside us, and what does it tell us about our nature? Where does the monster come from?

## No Danger Ahead

*F.E.A.R.: False Evidence Appearing Real*
— Alcoholics Anonymous slogan

At times, everyone on earth feels unsure, unsafe, unprotected, at risk. These are normal emotions we all share, normal reactions not to actual physical dangers but to the threats we imagine. But in the extreme, they can immobilize us— making us feel almost literally "frozen" with fear—or enrage us, sending us into aggressive overdrive.

The businessman, after he's been mildly criticized in a meeting, leaves the conference room with his heart pounding and his head exploding with thoughts of revenge on the colleague who contradicted him. The job applicant sits by the phone feeling numb, too frozen to make the call to find out whether she's been accepted or rejected. The boy sees indifference in his father's eyes and wants to run from the room. The preacher gets angry and scornful when someone voices a different spiritual view. There is a mystery in these reactions: a mild criticism, an anticipation of rejection, a difference of opinion, and yet their bodies are reacting as though their lives are at risk. What danger are they really facing?

There's a saying in Alcoholics Anonymous that F-E-A-R stands for "False Evidence Appearing Real." The fact is that most of our fears have no real danger, no real threat, connected to them. They are only mental events, with no objective facts to support them. But this doesn't keep us from being affected by them. Perceiving threat even when there is no threat, our hardwired biological instinct to survive sets off an elaborate alarm system in our bodies and minds, triggering physical responses—cardiovascular, muscular, biochemical, and neurological changes—that we experience as very real indeed.

## The Cause of Fear

> *And so, from hour to hour, we ripe and ripe,*
> *And then, from hour to hour, we rot and rot,*
> *And thereby hangs a tale.*
> — Shakespeare, *As You Like It*

It's well-known that our hardwired response to stress, originally designed to preserve our physical safety in a world full of predators, can play havoc with our well-being in the kinds of threatening situations modern life presents. A rush of adrenaline may have enabled prehistoric man to give a saber-toothed tiger the slip, but the executive in the meeting room does not benefit from tensed muscles and a racing heart. At first glance, then, it looks as if our survival instinct is out of sync with reality. But this isn't true. It is reacting to a deeper reality than the critical remark or the job interview: It is reacting to reality as it *really is*.

Our survival instinct is operating from a primal truth: that life is a wondrous and strange experience in which everything and everyone you see, including yourself, is subject to change and loss at any moment. This is true for every living being without exception. No religion grants you an exemption, and no amount of money or status can change the fact of your essential vulnerability in this world. This is Buddhism's "truth of impermanence." This, what Freud called "our helplessness," is the defining characteristic of the human condition: that we live with the awareness of our mortality.

Psychiatrist Aaron Beck, the pioneering founder of cognitive therapy, views the awareness of death as the root of all our anxieties: "In understanding anxiety, we should think of the symptoms not as foreign experiences but as expressions of basic, primal functions." The monsters that come to take children away in the night are storybook models of the truth that one day you and I will be taken from our present lives. And before we are taken, we will witness it happening to others, including those we love.

Looking at it in this light, we see that our fears are not unreasonable after all.

## Knowing Our Vulnerability

> *He who can look at the loveliness of the world,*
> *and share its sorrow, and realize something of*
> *the wonder of both, is in immediate contact*
> *with divine things.*
>
> — Oscar Wilde

While we share our vulnerable condition with all other living beings, our human capacity for self-awareness adds to its impact. As the poet Wendell Berry put it, we live with the "forethought of grief." We can't be sure, but we may be the only creatures on earth who go about our lives knowing that one day we won't be here.

Some people have a higher degree of sensitivity to this truth than others; they are more finely attuned to the possibility of change and loss and feel it more deeply. For many people, the end of summer is just the start of autumn, but for the sensitive ones it brings a melancholy as the light and heat give way to cooler days and earlier dark: the passing of the season touches in them an awareness of the passing of time and the inevitable ending of things. This kind of melancholy is not depression, but a deep movement of feeling that is distinct but beyond words. When Spanish flamenco or Portuguese fado singers let out their characteristic minor-key wails, they are giving voice to that feeling moving in them. I once heard a flamenco singer say that every one of his songs was a lamentation on the inevitability of loss.

We begin to sense the possibility of change and loss even as children, and some children are sensitive to it in their own way, asking intuitive and profound questions at a very young age about where people or pets go after they die. A few weeks after the death of her great-grandmother, whom we called GG, our 3-year-old granddaughter came up to me while I was raking leaves and asked very casually, "Is my GG dead?"

I answered, "Yes, sweetheart, she's dead."

Then she asked me if my mother was dead, and I said yes.

She was quiet for a moment, and then she asked me if my father was dead. I answered yes again, and I wished in that moment that I could see into the heart of her questions to grasp where she was going.

She then announced with confidence, "GG's not dead—she died."

That stopped my raking, and we sat down on the pile of leaves together.

I assumed she was just getting confused with her language, and so I modified her words and said them back to her: "Yes, love, she died, and now she's dead."

For the moment, she had nothing more to say. I gave her a hug, and she threw some leaves up into the air and went off to play in the garden.

A week later, while I was driving her to the day care

center, out of the blue she made exactly the same comment that GG had died but wasn't dead. This time, I just agreed with her, feeling that it was my time to say no more and to wonder what my granddaughter was trying to get across to me.

Her dog, a big old yellow Labrador retriever named Cody, had died a few months before GG. When my granddaughter asked her parents where Cody was, they told her he had gone to heaven. As I pulled into the day care center parking lot, she suddenly remarked that she'd had a dream about Cody; he and GG were playing together in heaven, and GG was very happy.

That matter-of-fact report seemed to put the question of GG's condition to rest. A few weeks later, as my granddaughter and I were walking in an apple orchard on a local farm, we spotted a big yellow Lab far down at the end of a row of apple trees. She didn't hurry toward him or even call out to him. She just said, "Look, Cody's back. Now he's with the farmers."

I agreed with her, and I wondered if she'd worked out in her little mind that one day GG, too, would be returning. I didn't believe in such things, but what did I know? Every speculation about life after death, even that there is none, is only speculation.

Adolescence usually brings a respite from such questioning, replacing it with the feeling that we are untouchable and immortal. This is a stage of development in which we sometimes behave recklessly without a second thought. It is also a stage in which our feelings of vulnerability are often buffered by self-righteous anger at the impositions of adults and authority in general. This angry certainty in our thoughts and feelings gives us, as teenagers, protection against the shifting complexity of our own moods and sense of self.

The reprieve, though, tends to be brief. Life makes us grow up fast, and soon enough we are introduced to our real situation. We experience the illness and death of friends and relatives; we begin to see signs of physical change in ourselves. Despite sometimes heroic mental efforts, in time we come face-to-face with our uncertain and temporary situation in this world. If we're not yet ready or able to confront it, we take refuge from it in one of several ways: in the supposed security of material success, in the comfort of religious faith, in the safe distance of detachment. But eventually we realize that we have to leave our refuge and look for real answers.

The need for real answers has grown exponentially with the awareness of the real problems we are facing in our social, political, health and environmental world. This search is especially active and even urgent in our adolescents and young adults who can view life globally more than any generation before them. They know, as has happened recently, that an uncontrolled forest fire on the west coast can drift heavy smoke all the way to the East coast. They know the statistics on the loss of species and have enough media exposure to our "leaders" to see those who offer manipulative and even sociopathic presentation of "facts." The list goes on, but the central point is that adolescents and young adults, as our future, need ways to stay in balance and search for new answers.

One evening, a man walked into my office and told me he needed an answer before he could go any further in his life. The human condition had become too real for him.

*The discovery takes something away*
*but puts nothing new in its place,*
*and so it sets in motion the search for*
*something new, something more.*

# 2

## The Material World

*Midway on the journey of our life,*
*I woke to find myself in a dark wood.*

— Dante

It was a cold winter night with a snowstorm predicted. I was tired and anxious to go home as I waited for my last appointment, a new patient named Ryan whom I'd never met before.

Ryan came into the office red-faced from the wind. As soon as he sat down, he woke me up with a startling question: "In one word, what's wrong with me, Doc?"

His question sounded like a demand. He was big and strong, with the air of a man used to being in charge of people and situations—which it turned out he was, as a highly paid sports-marketing executive. While he granted me a few moments to come up with my answer, he glanced around the office, and I saw him grimace as he spotted a statue of a meditating monk and a Botticelli print of Mary holding the infant Jesus. But as we began to talk, he dropped his managerial pose and became just another person like the rest of us, trying to figure life out.

Ryan had been struggling with anxious feelings and a nervous stomach for almost a year. He had gone to his doctor and to specialists, had tests that showed nothing wrong, and gotten prescriptions for tranquilizers he didn't want to take. Then, at his wife's urging, he had begun to search for answers from alternative practitioners and practices, including a well-known psychic, yoga classes, a nutritionist, and now a psychotherapist, me. He'd hoped for a quick fix from the psychic but was too skeptical to take her seriously; he spent the yoga classes sneaking glances at the young women in their formfitting yoga clothes; and he tried but couldn't follow the diet the nutritionist gave him.

He paused in his comic description of his search for a cure, very deliberately looked again at my monk statue, and rolled his eyes. "And now I'm sitting with some religious shrink who's going to tell me I'm nuts."

I thought it might work: "Okay, you're nuts."

Ryan got it and laughed, and then relaxed into his chair and told me his story with more genuine feeling.

He remembered the night his troubles began. He woke

at that inauspicious hour of 3 A.M. from a dream of being trapped in a building that seemed to have no exits. He was relieved to find that it was just a dream, but he had a hard time going back to sleep. He finally dozed off around 5 A.M.

When the alarm went off at 7, Ryan noticed feelings that he'd never had on any other morning. Usually he was glad to get up—on a weekday, because he enjoyed his job, and on weekends, because he looked forward to hanging out at home. But now he felt anxious; his stomach was jumpy, uneasy. He decided it was the result of a bad night's sleep, or maybe he was just coming down with a mild flu.

That afternoon at work, about to make a phone call to a well-known professional athlete, the kind of call he'd made hundreds of times before, he felt unusually nervous. Again, his stomach was part of the problem, so he figured he was definitely getting sick.

But the bad night's sleep and the nervous day were the beginning of a journey for Ryan. His symptoms became more frequent, showing up even when he was resting at home. He began to feel unpredictable to himself. Though he hated to do it, he called his doctor to schedule a checkup.

## The Symbolic Birthday

*Becoming engrossed in practical pursuits and personal duties can easily lead to isolation and to an unwarranted affirmation of the personal "I"…*

—Roberto Assagioli

As the wind-driven snow began hitting my office window, Ryan described his life to me. On the surface, it looked privileged, even blessed. As a boy he had loved sports, and now he was a successful executive in the sports industry, dealing with well-known athletes on an almost daily basis. His two children, both healthy, were impressed with the stars their father met and loved the special events they got to attend through his connections. His wife was attractive and supportive and a good mother.

What was wrong with this picture? There was no history of abuse in Ryan's childhood, no drug or alcohol addiction, no dark secrets. There was just one thing: he was 49 years old, which meant he was about to be 50.

I have seen such symbolic birthdays bring on the crisis of vulnerability all by themselves. Turning 50 sends the message that we have lived half our life—perhaps a little less than half, if we're very long-lived, but probably quite a bit more. And turning 60 hits even harder with the plain numerical fact that absolutely positively we have lived *much more than* half our life. There is no way, even in our wildest fantasy, that we are going to live to be 120 years old! Life no longer stretches out into an endless horizon of possibilities. The way things are is the way they're likely to stay. And the adolescent's assumption of immortality is a thing of the distant past: we know enough people who have fallen ill, enough people who have died, that it's undeniable it will happen to us too. Symbolic birthdays drive home the point that we live on borrowed time.

## Is This It?

> *Were there none who were discontented with what they have, the world would never reach anything better.*
>
> — Florence Nightingale

As Ryan approached 50, new questions had come up that he had never asked himself before, and they demanded answers. Was there something about the way he'd been living that had worked him into this anxious state? Had he made some big mistake that was going to come back to haunt him? Had he abandoned something important about himself that he used to care about a long time ago?

If just two years ago he'd heard other people talking like this, Ryan would have laughed. He'd have thought they were wasting their time when it was obvious that life was for living in the moment, seeking out new experiences, and achieving your goals, not for sitting around and ruminating over pointless questions. But now the questions had a new urgency, and there was one in particular that wouldn't leave him alone: "Is this it?"

When Ryan asked me that, I saw in my memory the faces of past patients who had asked the same thing. I knew that *this* referred to the present life the patient was leading, and that *it* implied something missing, something not enough, in this present life. The question seemed to come from a place in the self where we know that there is more, though we can't say exactly what that "more" might be.

This was certainly true for Ryan: even as he asked the question out loud, he said he didn't know what he was talking about. But he definitely felt it. The years were slipping away, time was passing by, and something had not yet happened that was supposed to happen. He knew what it wasn't—a business opportunity or a change in his personal life—but he couldn't pinpoint what it *was.* Sometimes he told himself to ignore the feeling and get on with the life he has. But the feeling, the longing for something more, wouldn't go away. It's one thing to hear about this longing, this "missing out" feeling, from someone who has never had a chance to experience life's sweetness. It's quite another thing to hear it from someone like Ryan, who has all the family and money and material possessions and professional status he needs to be content. To go even further up the ladder of material success, I've heard *Is this it?* from a man who has just built a grand home in the mountains with his Wall Street bonus, from a woman who has just returned from Hollywood with an Oscar. It tells me that the question's quiet power arises regardless of the facts of someone's life; it comes from a part of him or her deep inside that is indifferent to the outer reality.

At first Ryan had no idea where the question was coming from. What was he missing? What was so incomplete in his work or home life that it was making him ill? As we talked, a new level of his trouble began to reveal itself. He phrased it in particularly American terms: "I'm just not happy." I say "American" because it is the American myth that we are supposed to be happy, that the measure of our life is whether we are happy or not. Our Constitution even gives us the inalienable right to the pursuit of happiness. (Its writers were wise to say "the pursuit," suggesting how elusive happiness actually is.)

For Ryan, to say he was not happy was quite an admission. He had everything he could want, and yet it wasn't enough. Where does anyone go from there? He wanted to blame his parents, arguing that they had shown him a joyless existence full of complaining, but he was smart enough to know that blaming them was a dead end. He had to take responsibility himself. The thing that wouldn't let him be happy was something in his own way of living—something in *him*.

## The Buddha's Beginning

*Nothing is secure but life, transition, the energizing spirit.*

—Ralph Waldo Emerson

A few meetings later, Ryan was much closer to the source of his trouble. With an almost childlike innocence, he looked at me and said, "We all fucking die."

Death had been on his mind, it turned out, but he had kept pushing it away. He hadn't wanted to tell me about his thoughts of death because he was concerned that he'd be giving them too much credence. When they first came, he feared that someplace in the back of his mind he had a death wish or might even be contemplating suicide. But he didn't relate to such feelings; he could never imagine ending his own life and, far from wishing to die, hoped to live as long as possible. The real meaning of his thoughts was different: they were premonitions of his own death.

By the age of 49, Ryan had had enough life experience to see that even the good things in life come and go. He'd gotten enough phone calls in the middle of the night with the shocking news of someone's tragedy; he'd seen enough relationships end, projects collapse, and companies go bankrupt, and even several wars begin. He knew that life was unpredictable and that wanting it to be otherwise was wishful thinking. He had accepted these observations about life as truth, but truth in the abstract. Until now, he had successfully avoided applying them to himself.

Now he was beginning to do so. Something had gotten through to him—some combination of his symbolic birthday approaching, of hearing about things that were happening to his peers, or of moments when he felt less energy and strength than he used to—that led him to allow death more fully into his thinking. It was never clear to him or to me what single thing had opened the door; but one year ago his vulnerability had walked into his bedroom at 3 A.M. and he was forced to know it as his own.

Knowing didn't make it easy to accept that life would really end one day. It was painful to come out of the pleasant haze of ignorance many of us live in, in which our individual lives are exempt from the fate of all other people.

One of Ryan's first reactions to grasping his newfound vulnerability was anger at the way life is set up. "Is God some kind of sadist?" he asked me with absolute seriousness.

And the questions kept coming, the questions people have always asked as soon as the door opens and they see their own impermanence clearly. What is the point of life if we die and everything goes away? Why even bother to live a good life? Couldn't Ryan just cut loose from his obligations and do whatever he felt like? Since he was going to die anyway, what did it matter how he lived?

His questioning, his fears, weren't only for himself. As he absorbed the truth that all life is vulnerable, he saw his children through new eyes. He saw them as temporary, and it shocked him. As a parent, he'd already marveled at the changes and stages of development children go through— how quickly the years passed—but now he was taking in the *end* of his children's lives.

Intellectually, of course, Ryan had known all this before. Now it was different: he was feeling it. Every instinct in him was telling him to stop thinking this way, to run away from these terrible thoughts as fast as he could, but something deeper than his fear was telling him to stay put. It was telling him he had stumbled upon something that mattered. He had connected his anxiety to its source in his innate vulnerability; now he needed a way to integrate this bare truth of life.

Ryan had made the same discovery that shocked Prince Siddhartha—the Buddha—out of his privileged, sheltered life and into sudden clarity when he saw three people, one old, one sick, one dead. Siddhartha had never before grasped that sickness, old age, and death were humanity's inescapable fate—in fact, he'd been shielded from even knowing that they existed. He hurried to his father for an explanation, but his father had none, so the prince left his happy life and set out on a spiritual search for an answer to this same bare truth.

He sought answers first in religion, renouncing all of his worldly possessions and going into the forest to lead an ascetic life with a group of wandering monks. Eating little, forcing himself to sit in meditation hour after hour, he tried to escape his vulnerability by denying his body's needs. When years of this brought him no closer to answers, he went in the opposite direction. He began to live only for today, plunging into materialism and hedonism; he became an associate of a wealthy businessman and even indulged his sensuality with a prostitute. In time this second choice, too, proved empty, and he continued on the path to a third choice—a "middle way" of balance and insight that would become the basis of one of the world's great spiritual traditions.

## Something New, Something More

*Hope…allows the movement from being to becoming, which is possible at every moment of human existence.*

—Cathleen Fanslow

Ryan was only at the beginning of his journey. Like the Buddha, he had had to abandon his old idea of life as something that stretched out into the limitless horizon. He felt less comfortable in his time-limited body, clearly just a temporary rental. Life had closed in—a door had shut—and he sensed its limits with new urgency.

I have come to think of changes like this as discoveries of "negative knowledge." Even though your knowledge of reality has expanded, the result is that you are left with less. The discovery takes something away but puts nothing new in its place, and so it sets in motion the search for something new, something more, to fill the gap.

What had been taken away from Ryan? I realized that his confrontation with his vulnerability had shattered his faith in his religion. Not Christianity, Judaism, Buddhism, Islam, Hinduism, Taoism, or any other traditional religion; his faith had been in materialism, in the aggressive acquiring of the objects and rewards of this world. Ryan didn't just participate in materialism as a practical matter, as we all must—a compromise we make to get money for food, shelter, and other necessities. He shaped his life around it, believed in it as the road to happiness, and hoped to instill its values in his children.

I link materialism with the religions of the world because it looks a lot like one. It has tenets and adherents just like any established sect. The religion of materialism is the ardent belief in the world of objects, the world you can see with your eyes, and the equally ardent desire to experience as much of this world—to enjoy and own as many of its objects—as possible. It has priests who convince you that you need these objects and places of worship where you go to buy them.

In this world of objects, a believing materialist views himself as just another object. He compares himself objectively to others in terms of the numbers in their bank accounts, the prices of their cars and houses, their status in the workplace or the community, and some of his suffering comes from knowing that they have more than he. He may even treat his body as an object, subjecting it to extremes of exercise or surgery in the hope of making it look better to others. Caught up in the appearances of the visible world, he is equally caught up in his own appearance and the way he believes others see him.

Then the day comes when it dawns on the materialist that the things he has been depending upon to make him happy can't possibly produce happiness. To fight off such dangerous knowledge, at first he relies on them even more. This is the stereotypical "midlife crisis," which in our culture has been made into a desperate joke: the picture of the middle-aged man acting out his fear of age and time by dating much younger women, driving a flashy car, or trying to be the athlete he never was. But though the behaviors can be comical, we shouldn't let that obscure what drives them: a deep awareness of vulnerability.

Here was Ryan, a man living in prosperity and thriving on materialism, and yet he was full of sadness and fear. The human condition had revealed itself to him, and now he needed something new, something more, to live by.

*Sensitive ones are those who are so*
*highly attuned to the inherent,*
*inevitable fact of change and loss in this life.*

# 3

## Belief and Disbelief

*Whatever satisfies souls is true.*

— Walt Whitman

Ryan's crisis came upon him while he was lying in his own bed in the middle of the night. Barbara's hit her in an even more unlikely place—while she was sitting peacefully in her church.

The priest was giving a sermon of the kind Barbara had gladly listened to many times before, but this time she felt herself cringing at his statements. She caught herself doing it several times, and she hoped no one had noticed. Impatient and restless, she was relieved when the priest finally stopped talking. She looked around the beautiful church that was so much a part of her life. And then the crisis came: In a quiet, certain thought, she knew that she didn't believe in any of it anymore.

Why was this happening to her? And why now? Recently retired from her long career as a school librarian, Barbara was looking forward to a life of leisure and pleasant diversions. She was happily married, with two grown children and one grandchild whom she adored; her future spread out like a long series of family gatherings, trips to interesting places, and a daily life free from the demands of any schedule.

But so far it hadn't played out the way she'd envisioned. Instead, over six months' time, Barbara's husband's beloved sister had fallen ill and died; then her mother had fallen and broken her hip, undergone hip replacement surgery, moved into a nursing care center for rehabilitation, and then died.

On the night of her mother's surgery, lying in bed, Barbara had the first major anxiety attack of her life. She had been a worrier since her teens, but she'd never experienced anything like the horrible, overwhelming dread the attack brought on. She crawled under the covers and stayed there until the fear subsided. More symptoms followed: Barbara began to experience shooting pains in her neck and back, and she was constantly on the alert for any feelings that suggested another anxiety attack starting up. Within half a year's time, life as she'd known it—and expected it to be—was taken away from her.

Until she became so ill with anxiety, Barbara had been deeply involved in her Catholicism. Not only had she attended church regularly, she'd been a eucharistic minister, giving out Communion at Mass. But as she tried to cope with her pains and the dread of another attack, she no longer felt as though her beliefs were helping her. For her this was an intimate loss, and it cut deep: she felt personally abandoned by God.

For months she had tried responding to her anxiety and grief by plunging even more deeply into faith. She went to Mass every day, prayed often, and even joined a prayer group made up of extremely devout Catholics who placed all their hopes in God's benevolent protection. The group's intense religiosity disturbed Barbara, but she tolerated it because they insisted that Jesus would cure her. Eventually, though, when her suffering didn't abate, she spoke to her doctor, who sent her for what seemed like every known medical test to pinpoint the source of her pains. When all the tests proved negative, which meant that no physical cause could be found, she called me to learn how to meditate.

## A Sensitive One

*Heartbreak is a treasure because*
*it contains mercies.*
*The kernel is soft when the*
*rind is scraped off.*

— Rumi

I liked Barbara immediately. She was warm and open, she looked me in the eye, and, like Ryan, she bravely tried to be humorous about "going crazy." But the stress she felt just from sitting in an office and telling her story to a stranger was palpable.

After a short time I showed her a meditation technique based on the Chinese healing system of Qi Gong, which my wife and I had studied for years, to help her get some relief. I guided her to place one hand on her belly, then the other hand on top of the first, and to notice the sensation of her belly rising and falling with her breath. Within three minutes she felt significantly more relaxed, but she also told me that she had difficulty letting go. She was concerned that relaxing might not be such a good idea.

As we talked this out, Barbara realized that part of her was *afraid* to relax, because if she relaxed she wouldn't be scanning so vigilantly for signs of the next anxiety attack. I asked her if she had been this vigilant before the attacks started happening, and at first she said no. But on reflection, she admitted that part of her had always been on watch for something bad happening to her or the people she cared about. She had been living "poised for danger."

Now I saw in Barbara one of the sensitive ones we described in Chapter 1, those people who are so highly attuned to the inherent, inevitable fact of change and loss in this life. I speculated that she had probably never told anyone about her sensitivity because she thought that everyone else was handling life just fine. That was right, she said, startled. Then I startled her even more by telling her that her lifelong sensitivity to loss was an accurate and realistic appreciation of life as life is.

I explained that her sensitivity placed her in a special club with members around the world (myself being one of them)—people who couldn't ignore or deny the difficult parts of reality and were more susceptible than most to the passing of time and the inexorable process of change. Barbara's face lit up with recognition. She said, "That's why I've been searching for something my whole life."

## Leaving the Refuge

> *I would like to beg you to have patience with*
> *everything unresolved in your heart and try to*
> *love the questions themselves.*
>                             — Rainer Maria Rilke

Barbara's search had led her, early on, to a deep commitment to her religion, and that commitment had lasted throughout her adult life. She'd built her faith on an idea of God as all-powerful and protective, caring for her and watching over her—an idea many believers share. In this view, if something good happens, it is because God has willed it to happen. If something bad happens, God has willed that, too, and the badness of the experience is God's way of trying to help or teach you: even in the badness, God is protecting you. Nothing happens without God being part of it. Change, loss, and death happen, yes—but they are all happening within God's world, so there is ultimately nothing to fear. It is a supremely attractive view, one that captivates the hearts and minds of hundreds of millions around the world.

But it only lasts as long as you can continue to believe in this benevolent God, and some realities tend to erode our belief. Working in the oncology unit of a major medical center for four years—including the children's cancer ward—I walked in and out of many rooms of intense suffering where I saw no heavenly protection at work. In one case, a prominent minister lost his faith when he fell into despair over his illness, and I saw his visiting parishioners leave his hospital room shaken by his bitterness and sense of abandonment. On a grander scale, Christianity suffered a dramatic decline in Europe after World War II, when the deaths of over 40 million people posed a terrible challenge to faith in a protective God.

Barbara's faith lasted until that quiet, certain moment in church when it became fully clear to her that she no longer believed in God's protective power to save her from suffering. Up to this point, Barbara had refused to entertain any doubts about her religion. Now she was letting in thoughts that were dismantling it altogether. In the past she had been glad to believe that her religion contained eternal truths; now she was stepping back and taking in the fact that, after all, her religion was the invention of men, and that in the course of its history those "eternal" truths had been adjusted and altered many times.

## Going Beyond Belief

> *People wish to be settled; only as far as they are*
> *unsettled is there any hope for them.*
> —Ralph Waldo Emerson

The change in her thinking felt cataclysmic to Barbara. But when she finally got up the courage to express her thoughts to someone—her husband, David—he just looked at her with bemused curiosity. For years David, a skeptic by nature, had put up with his wife's piety only because it seemed so important to her. He let himself be dragged to church on the major religious holidays, but otherwise he avoided the place like the dentist's office. He was glad to hear Barbara's new doubts, and he encouraged her to keep questioning.

Deep down, David felt that Barbara's religion had lulled her into a fantasy. It pleased him to think that she would no longer waste her time on answers that were bound to disappoint her in the end. Unfortunately, he had no idea what new answers could take their place. As a skeptic, he was most skilled at scrutinizing and rejecting ideas. He didn't know what he believed in, but he knew with certainty what he didn't believe and couldn't accept. Perhaps he didn't believe in anything at all.

But skeptics like David do, in fact, have strong beliefs: They believe in the religion of their own minds. A skeptic puts all his trust in his own thinking to come up with the truth about life. He will know it is the real truth because it will have passed the test of his own scathing doubts and challenges. He trusts that his mental process is rational and objective, in contrast to the wishy-washy, self-deluded thinking of others; of course, he is often deluded in this himself, since his own values and emotional needs invariably influence his thinking. He wants only the truth, and that is admirable; the problem is that his version of the truth is limited to what his mind is capable of comprehending. And his truth is no more immune than other systems of belief— faith in material things, trust in a benevolent God—to collapsing under the weight of real life.

## The Limits of Reason

*We dip our fingers in the sea that would make*
*us invulnerable if we would plunge and swim.*
— Ralph Waldo Emerson

Miriam was a 76-year-old woman who had started drinking heavily after the death of her husband four years earlier. Up till then, she had been a social drinker, but in her changed life as a widow she felt lonely and vulnerable, and alcohol became a consolation and a medication. One night, after drinking two bottles of wine, she tried to open a third bottle, but it fell and shattered on the kitchen floor. The next morning, feeling hung over and sick, with no memory of the shattered bottle from the night before, she walked into the kitchen and stepped on a big piece of broken glass. That afternoon, she called the local hospital's drug and alcohol recovery program and was admitted to the detox unit. That's where she met my wife.

Bonney, who was working there as a nurse psychotherapist, interviewed Miriam early in her stay to plan for further treatment after the detoxification. Thin and nervous, with sallow skin and dark circles under her eyes, Miriam seemed defeated and humiliated, but her mind was quick and acerbic. When Bonney asked her if she had made other attempts to stop drinking, she said that she'd once gone to Alcoholics Anonymous but was turned off by the talk of God. Her father and brother had died in World War II, killed in a Nazi concentration camp; after God had let that happen, she said, God was dead to her.

In describing her life as a widow, Miriam painted a picture of severe social isolation. Trying to get the full picture, Bonney asked her if she had any connection to a local synagogue. Miriam looked at Bonney as if she was crazy. Hadn't she just said that God was dead to her? "That's just a social club," she scoffed. "I bet those people don't believe anything anyway. How could they?"

After five days in detox, Miriam went home, "dried out"—she'd had no alcohol since she had been admitted. When she came in the next morning for her first outpatient session with Bonney, she already looked a little better; her skin had regained some color and she'd had a decent night's sleep. But Bonney knew that Miriam would face a challenge in dealing with her twin compulsions—the physical craving for alcohol and the emotional need to have that old companion back in her life. Trying to learn of any resources Miriam could draw on in her recovery, Bonney asked again if she had any spiritual practice or perspective. She was assuming that the horror of the Holocaust would have forced Miriam to seek solace and meaning somewhere. But Miriam flinched at Bonney's question and answered angrily, "If you're naïve enough to talk to me about synagogue and spirituality, then I don't think you can help me."

In fact, Miriam *had* found meaning—not in a belief system, but in the refuge of her own disbelief. She had always relied on her mind to defend her from the truth of human vulnerability that she'd been exposed to in such a devastating form. But now her thoughts could no longer show her a way through the oppression of all the loss in her life. Later, she would tell Bonney that it humiliated her to reveal her problems to a stranger in this way—to admit that her mind had failed her—and that, at this point, she really couldn't think of any reason to live.

Where do you turn when your primary defense has left you and the answers it gave you have failed? In my view, you turn toward the question that is driving you to look for answers in the first place. Joining Ryan, Barbara, Miriam, and many others to come, we'll now begin to approach, appreciate, and ultimately transform our fears.

# PART II

transforming fear

*It is understandable, and moving, that we wish for someone in our life who can help us with our fear, uncertainty, and unhappiness.... But how can it truly work when what you are hoping for from me is what I am hoping for from you?*

# 4

## From Denial to Decision

*The Over-Soul*
*The wise silence, the universal beauty*
*To which every part and particle is*
*equally related, is the tide of being which*
*floats us into the secret of nature and*
*we stand before the secret of the world.*

— Ralph Waldo Emerson

Until we realize that our fears originate in our own awareness of inevitable change and loss, we blame them on causes outside us, convinced that other people, places, and things are making us feel vulnerable and threatened. It is perfectly clear why we do this; we couldn't function if we walked around with too much understanding of the real, inner cause. We would be either too depressed by its hopelessness or too caught up in nervously scanning our surroundings for signs of imminent danger. Living with the full awareness of our actual human condition would render us "crippled for action," as the author Ernest Becker put it in his Pulitzer Prize–winning book, *Denial of Death.* "The individual has to protect himself against . . . the terrors of the world and . . . his own anxieties," Becker wrote. "The essence of normality is the refusal of reality."

Becker wrote this while he was dying of cancer and seeking answers to his own fears. His terminal diagnosis made his own "refusal of reality" impossible to maintain. His vulnerability crashed in on him, destroying his own denials; his brave book is a testament to a highly intelligent mind working full-time to make sense of his impermanence— and, by extension, ours.

Until we face a crisis like Becker's—or some other situation that brings reality crashing in on us—we instinctively push the vulnerability of our actual human condition out of our awareness so we can live with a sense that we are solid and stable and not be "crippled for action." However, the cost of hiding the truth from ourselves is high. In this chapter, we'll look at a couple of the ways we deny our vulnerability, and we'll observe the harm they can do us. But we'll also start to see how we can turn them around if we decide to stop denying.

## The Hidden Hope in Relationships

*Passing stranger! You do not know*
*how longingly I look upon you.*
*You must be he I was seeking,*
*or she I was seeking . . .*
*I have somewhere surely lived*
*a life of joy with you*

— Walt Whitman

Joe had just gotten home from work and was relaxing on the couch, ready to watch the local news on TV. When he came in, he'd shouted his greeting of hello to his wife, Jean, assuming she was somewhere in the apartment, but had heard nothing back. But now, with bad timing, just as Joe clicked the TV on, Jean emerged from the bedroom with a dour look on her face.

Half looking at her and half looking at the TV screen lighting up, Joe asked flatly, "What?"

Jean felt hurt because Joe sounded so annoyed, but she suppressed her hurt as best she could and said, "Never mind."

Her reply angered Joe because, first, she interrupted him as he was about to relax, and then, second, she wouldn't even tell him why she was interrupting him. With vehemence in his voice, he asked her again, "What?!"

*What? Never mind. What?!* This was a representative

conversation for Jean and Joe, one of so many disappointing, hurtful, and angry attempts at communication. Like the majority of marriages in America, this one was also headed for divorce, though Jean and Joe hadn't used the word yet. In time, after all the goodwill had been drained out of their relationship and they'd both began to actively fantasize about getting away from the other, they came to me briefly for couples counseling. I heard the *What? Never mind. What?!* story from them as an iconic tale of the frustration of so many unhappy, uncared-for couples I'd seen in my professional practice.

My few unsuccessful counseling sessions with Jean and Joe were attempts to resuscitate a relationship that had already passed away. What had died? The capacity to care about, or even be interested in, each other's vulnerable feelings.

Joe had long ago given up on Jean's ability to help him with his work anxieties. She just didn't seem to think that his struggles mattered. She'd yawn while he was talking, she'd change the subject, she'd wonder out loud if they could go out to dinner rather than cook. He was trying to explain, yet again, some hidden motive in his boss's comments or actions, but Jean didn't seem to get the importance of it.

Joe was mystified: How could she not care, or at least try to understand? He made more money than she did, and his job was connected to their mutual economic survival. Did she think he was so thrilled with his work? Did she think he really wanted to spend so much energy thinking and talking about it? Not knowing what to do for a career early in his life, he'd fallen into this line of administrative work years ago, even though he was never really suited for it. But now, this particular job was crucial because Joe dreaded the thought of having to look for new work, a situation in which it felt to him as if he would be begging someone for a chance and setting himself up to be rejected. He was still haunted by the anxious job-seeking process he'd gone through before he'd found his current position.

He had described all of these doubts and fears to Jean in great detail, and so he was particularly sensitive to the times when she cut the conversation short by telling him to just quit and go look for a new job. To Joe, this was even further proof of her indifference to his anxieties and vulnerabilities.

For Jean's part, she had eventually become bored to death with Joe's compulsive analyses of his boss's every word and motive. When Jean read between the lines of Joe's descriptions, the boss sounded neither better nor worse than bosses Jean had had and had heard about from friends. She was disappointed by Joe's inability to rise above his nervousness and to get beyond his fixation on how the boss's every interaction was threatening and portentous. To Jean's mind, the boss was either a skilled sadist or, more likely, a stand-in for some frightening authority figure from Joe's childhood. In either case, she had lost respect for Joe because of his complaining and worrying, and she resented the fact that his anxieties had made *her* a more anxious person than she used to be.

In addition, his compulsive worrying sucked all of the oxygen out of the room and gave her little space to speak about her own vulnerabilities. When she walked out of the bedroom that evening with a dour look on her face, she had just heard bad news about a friend who'd gotten a diagnosis of breast cancer. She had a need to talk about it, but Joe's clicking on the TV was a signal that he wasn't interested in listening to her. The breast cancer diagnosis had of course stirred up her own deep fears, but all she'd gotten from her supposed partner, lover, and best friend was "What?!"

It is understandable, and moving, that we wish for someone in our life who can help us with our fear, uncertainty, and unhappiness. Relationships, especially romantic ones, bear a silent but intense pressure to relieve us in our difficult times of vulnerability. It is in these relationships that we lower our defenses, admit to our secret hopes and deepest fears, and open ourselves to our shared human hope for unqualified support and true friendship. Since we don't usually realize that the source of our vulnerability is in our own nature, in our very human condition, we look outside ourselves to our partners, yearning for signs that they will know how to provide this essential security for us. But how can it truly work when what you are hoping for from me is what I am hoping for from you?

*"I'm just not happy,"* say the people who haven't found out what it is in themselves that drives their longing and increases their unhappiness. Without this self-knowledge, we are fated to keep looking for the solution to our vulnerabilities in other people, places, and things, be it the dreamy promise of new relationships, fantasies of escape to a trouble-free life, or the satiating possession of everything we have ever wanted.

## Crossing the Bridge

> *Perhaps everything that frightens us is, in its deepest essence, something helpless that wants our love.*
>
> — Rainer Maria Rilke

This doesn't have to happen. No couple needs to turn into Jean and Joe. Our vulnerability need not be the thing that divides us; it's really the bridge that connects us. Any couple, even one with wildly different temperaments, can find this bridge.

I remember a couple for whom the bridge at first seemed hopelessly blocked. In the episodes of fear and tension that life inevitably brings, Frank would ignore his feelings and run to his mind to logically figure out the answer, while his wife, Rita, would become so upset that for a little while she couldn't think straight. When they got a call from the junior high school principal that their daughter had been caught smoking marijuana in the girls' bathroom, Frank began thinking out loud about whether he should call his lawyer friend for advice, while Rita looked as if she was going to throw up as she sobbed. In this time of crisis, like so many others in their married life, Frank judged his wife to be overreactive and useless, and in turn Rita judged her husband to be a cold fish who was completely out of touch with his feelings. They had each privately wondered many times how he or she had gotten stuck with someone who was so different.

Their daughter was suspended from school for two days and, though legal action wasn't a threat, the school wanted her to get counseling. Because I was known to work with issues of addiction and recovery, Rita and Frank came to consult with me about their daughter's trouble. As they were recounting the principal's first phone call, Rita began to tear up, and Frank turned on her: "Give me a break! You're going to start crying here, too, in front of this man?!"

Rita looked right into my eyes and announced with resignation, "He doesn't feel anything."

Looking at Frank, twisted up in his chair and staring at the door as if he was planning to escape from my office, I saw someone obviously wracked with feeling. I kept in mind that they had come for help on how to assess their daughter's involvement with drugs, but I saw the opportunity in the moment to bridge the gap between them, at least for the sake of working in unison on their daughter's situation.

Without looking at Frank, I said to Rita, "He looks pretty upset to me."

That was risky in two ways. Frank and I had no bond yet, and he could have taken my comment as intrusive, while Rita could have taken it, rightly, as correcting her opinion. I went for it anyway because the room was charged with emotions, and I wanted to find out what the emotions had to say.

Frank gave me a half-approval: "Anyone's going to be upset about something like this. The point is what to do about it."

I used a standard counseling technique that I'd learned early in graduate school, which always works: "Tell me more."

Without a pause, Frank did so. He told me about his daughter's intelligence and thoughtfulness and bright future, and he said that since she'd started junior high school he was beginning to think he didn't know her anymore. Previously verbal and forthcoming, she'd become moody and silent, giving one- or two-word answers to every question he asked.

Rita couldn't resist: "She tells *me* things."

Frank looked worried. "Like what?"

Our first meeting went on in this vein. While trying to stay on the subject of their daughter, Rita and Frank couldn't resist little digs back and forth over who was the better parent. Frank was concerned that their daughter was learning from Rita that it was all right to indulge your feelings and to go into semi-breakdowns over the simplest things, and Rita was concerned that their daughter was learning from Frank to shut down feelings and to go through life like a robot. But they weren't really debating the "better parent" award: the real purpose of their digs was to defend their very sense of self against attacks from the other. I told them we would need a second meeting and, to my surprise, they were both glad to set up another appointment.

In couples counseling, there is the early unspoken hope in each person that the therapist will judge him or her to be the one who is right and his or her partner to be wrong. I sensed that Rita and Frank had already cast me in the judge's role, but I wanted a second meeting to point them to the bridge that powerfully connected them: their fears about their daughter whom they both clearly loved.

I took on a very directive tack in the second meeting. Looking right at Rita, I explained to her that all of Frank's logic was an attempt to reduce the threat that had arisen in their family. I turned to Frank and explained that Rita's feelings were reflecting the degree of alarm that had been triggered by this surprising turn in their daughter's life. Then I told them as a couple that what Frank figures out logically and what Rita gathers emotionally are both valuable sources of information, and that these sources together create what any of us needs to make a good decision—a balance of mind and heart. I spelled it out, saying that if Frank could be curious about Rita's feelings and Rita curious about Frank's thoughts, they could synthesize their emotion and logic and come up with the right thing to do for their daughter in this time of trouble. I also told them that I had noticed Frank *having feelings* about what he was thinking and Rita *thinking* about how she felt, and so they weren't really that different and certainly didn't deserve the negative labels of the logical robot or the emotional wreck. Their difference was only in the initial reactions they had to threat, which sent Frank to his mind and Rita to her feelings.

I gave them the name of a female counselor whom their daughter could see as part of the school's requirement, and they seemed together and content when they left the meeting. Two months later, Frank called me up to thank me and to say that he'd been reading a popular book about how male and female gender differences manifest in relationships. He said that he and Rita had seen themselves with humor on every page.

The bridge of shared vulnerability, on this occasion stirred up by their daughter's trouble, had opened for them so that they could cross over to each other. They now had the insight that Frank used his thinking to reduce his fear, and that Rita used her emotions to discharge her fear, and that they could learn from each other's approaches and work as a team, rather than as two individuals feeling isolated and misunderstood in a time of crisis.

As we'll see in the next chapter, this bridge of shared vulnerability will also turn out to be an important step on *our* path together—our first practice in the transformation of fear.

## Soothing the Pain

> *The blue sky opens out farther and farther, the*
> *daily sense of failure goes away, the damage I*
> *have done to myself fades . . .*
> *when I sit firmly in the world.*
>
> — Kabir

When Rona was 11, her father died of a heart attack. It happened without warning, during the day, while he was at work. Rona's mother got the phone call with the shocking news and immediately went into protective mode to try to shield her sensitive child from the loss. She told Rona to go to her room and to stay there "until Mommy comes to get you."

Looking back, Rona remembered the sounds of relatives starting to come into the house and wondering in her young mind if a big party was about to begin. The relatives flocked around Rona's mother, giving her constant attention, and took charge of all the funeral arrangements, while Rona obediently sat in her room with her beloved dog. Every once in a while, her mother, looking very pale, popped her head in and told her that the adults had to talk about something very important, that Rona was to stay where she was. Rona now sensed that something really bad had happened, but she put on her radio and hugged her sweet dog as if she were hanging on to a life raft. The dog's warm body and long fur felt so soothing against Rona's chest, and she held him and held him. With the special sense that pets have, the dog sat still and let Rona cling.

As the months passed and Rona tried to cope with her grief, she sought out that physically soothing feeling again and again—sometimes from her pet, then sometimes from eating until she felt full and dulled. If she was alone in the house for more than a few minutes, she'd get uneasy, so she would go to the refrigerator to find whatever she could that was edible. By the time she came to me, Rona was 28 years old, living alone in the city, and she had an addiction to eating compulsively in order to soothe herself whenever she felt lonely or vulnerable.

The word *addiction* may conjure up the image of

someone using dangerous, illegal substances such as heroin. But if we think of what lies at the root of addiction—a compelling need inside a person to change bad feelings—we can see a broader picture, encompassing all the legal, doctor-prescribed mind- and mood-altering drugs so prevalent in our modern world. Anti-anxiety pills, antidepressants with an anti-anxiety component, sedatives, painkillers, muscle relaxants, stomach remedies, sleep aids—all are in greater demand than ever, and many people feel dependent on these pills for their well-being.

Beyond the doctor's office and the prescription pad, there are also millions of people acting as their own doctors, self-medicating with a whole pharmacopoeia of substances— marijuana, cocaine, crystal meth, hallucinogens, steroids— to make themselves feel better. There's also a vast array of herbal supplements that people take with little knowledge of the product quality or correct dosage. Then there's the number one self-administered medicine for the treatment of bad feelings: alcohol. Reports of alcohol use and abuse vary widely, but the best estimates indicate consistently that at any given time 18 million Americans are addicted to alcohol and that 53 percent of Americans have a drinking problem in the family. Finally, there are compulsions like Rona's: addictions to eating, gambling, dieting, exercising, shopping, the internet and other technologies that can be continuously present.

Bonney and I worked in rehabilitation centers for many years, and we came to see that all addictions—no matter how broadly we define the term—have the common aim of relieving, removing, or suppressing emotional pain. Patient after patient told us that he or she used drugs to get rid of feeling bad, feeling "less than," not feeling good enough to cope with life. Bonney in particular, in her work with heroin addicts from all walks of life, learned something even more revealing: she found that the great majority of them had experienced a significant loss early in their lives— abandonment, the death of a sibling, the death of a parent. These patients had been exposed early to the harsh reality of the human condition, without support to help them cope with the pain, which now arose in new forms in their bodies and emotions. She found, in other words, that they were turning to drugs to buffer their feelings of vulnerability in this world.

When we realize that drug use is medicine to treat feelings of fear and vulnerability, we can take the pointless moralizing out of the picture. Someone hooked on drugs is facing the same fear that we are, only with greater impediments and perhaps less emotional skill—and with an ongoing challenge. Once the drugs are out of his or her system, the person in recovery is left to cope once again with the essential vulnerability that led him or her into addiction in the first place, this time without the buffer. The success of his or her recovery will depend on finding newer, healthier ways to face the fear.

## The Decision

> *To explore spiritual crisis in this present day*
> *is far from being old fashioned or useful only*
> *as an academic exercise…It meets an urgent*
> *need…*
>
> — Roberto Assagioli

The same thing is true for each of us. Our reactions to the normal, natural fear within us determine the course of our life. At its worst, fear renders us "crippled for action"; at its best, fear becomes the path to our highest possibilities. The path begins when we learn how to approach and appreciate our fear and respond to it in a transformative way.

There is a part of me that wishes life wasn't like this. This dreamy, delusional part of me wants to believe that I will go through life in perfect health until my very old age, at which point my body will be so exhausted that I will see death as a vacation from the physical world, after which I will pass onto a metaphysical plane of bliss.

In this dream of a life, none of the people I love will suffer or have anything bad happen to them. Bad things will happen, of course—such is life—but they will happen only to other people, while I learn of them at a distance, in the newspaper or on television. In this dream of safety, I eat a sandwich and drink a beer in the comfort of my home while total strangers suffer on my TV screen.

Given a choice, I would prefer my delusion—except that it *is* a delusion. All I have written so far on the subject of our shared vulnerability boils down to a clear inner decision that you must make for yourself: Do you want to get through life in a dream of avoidance? Or do you want to be alive to life as it is?

*Our vulnerable reality, just as it is, with
no magical solutions or illusory protections,
opens the door to a deeper part of our mind
where boundaries dissolve and a unifying
love rules. This is the mind in oneness.*

# 5

## Strength in Surrender

*To be depriving death of its
greatest advantage over us,
let us adopt a way contrary to
the common one: let us
deprive death of its strangeness,
let us get used to it.*

— Montaigne

It was a summer evening, and the sun was still shining in my office window at 8 P.M. as Ryan sat across from me and waited for his answer.

Since our first meeting in the winter, Ryan had seen me only a few times, preferring to try to solve the puzzle of vulnerability by overriding his vulnerable feelings with sheer willpower and personal strength. From his recent choices, it seemed to me that he was actually tempting fate to force a confrontation with his vulnerability. He'd thrown himself into work with a crazed, hectic schedule including extra air travel far beyond what his senior role in the company required, and he had taken up, of all things, bungee jumping. He laughed so hard that he could barely talk as he gave me the picture of himself harnessed to a bungee cord, loaded up on the anti-anxiety pills his doctor had prescribed for him, ready to jump off a bridge. He was making it sound as if he'd gone crazy, and he enhanced this impression by describing his competing fantasies of divorcing his wife or moving his whole family to the wilderness—both strategies to drastically change his life so that he might feel whole again. He had even thought—briefly—of trying to become religious.

Where do you turn when your guiding principle has left you? I had no magic words for Ryan, even as he faced me across my office, waiting for relief. All I had for him was a path I had taken years ago. I started on the path after I'd given up on my own attempts to find an answer to vulnerability, when I began to realize that you don't look for an answer *to* it, you look for an answer *in* it.

## The Way of Vulnerability

> *More than a **wish**, of deeper origin than a*
> ***goal**, that thing called **hope** is actually what*

*drives the process of change…There is a reason*
*for the maxim, "hope springs eternal."*
—Cathleen Fanslow

Early in my life, long before I took up vulnerability as a subject, I erected my own barriers against it. I started building them during my preteen years living with a father who seemed to hate me. I appreciate now that he himself was highly vulnerable, having emigrated as a lonely young man with one piece of luggage to America, but at the time, all I experienced was his sarcasm and his coldness. I was his oldest son, but he appeared to be utterly uninterested in anything I said or did, and his only expression of emotion was the slam of a door somewhere in the house, announcing that he wanted to be left alone. My mother and brothers and I all got the message: we were not to seek him out or ask anything of him. It made supper time, the one time we were all usually in the room together, a slow torture of silences and dirty looks.

I don't remember making any clear decision to turn myself into someone who was detached. I just started acting that way, complete with an aloof facial expression. I was going to solve the dilemma of being hurt by ceasing to be vulnerable at all. Ironically, with no awareness on my part, I had come up with a way of protecting myself through a pose of indifference that was very much like the way my father treated me.

I relied on this protection through high school and college. I had friends, and I generally got along with people, but I retreated to detachment and indifference whenever someone or something touched a vulnerable nerve. If someone said something critical about me, for example, I escaped the pain by deciding I didn't care about him. When others got upset about an incident, I made sure to demonstrate with my comments that it wasn't affecting me.

Then I married Bonney, and she wouldn't let me be that way. Each time I struck my pose of detached indifference toward her, she openly cried, and my pose began to weaken. I didn't transform overnight into a compassionate, loving husband, but at least I was showing some emotion, even if at first it took the form of anger or distress at her crying. And when we had children, that was it—my bad plan of protection fell apart. When my daughter cut her finger, I felt the cut go viscerally through my whole body. When my son was picked on, I planned to kill the bully who was scaring him. When I myself was ill or hurt, it troubled me most that it caused my family trouble. My wife and my children had wrecked my sad little plan to go through life without being vulnerable.

I had hoped to live a detached life, but I didn't succeed, and I was glad. Each time I felt the force of vulnerability, and allowed myself to stay with it instead of escaping into detachment, I felt more human, more soulful, more real.

I was beginning to see that vulnerability was a conduit to a better life. Over time my resolve was challenged—when my parents died; when the rest of my older relatives died, leaving me the oldest surviving member of the family; when my good friend died at 49 of a brain aneurysm; when our son's childhood friend overdosed on heroin and died at 16; when a dear friend's daughter died of a virulent infection at 22 and left behind a 1-year-old child, and so many other losses—and I remember feeling seduced by my old plan of trying not to care. But fortunately for me, the conduit of vulnerability stayed open, and the losses made the world feel both more painful and more precious at the same time.

## Michelangelo's Mary

*A simple, quiet, undescribed, indescribable presence is dwelling peacefully in us.*
— Ralph Waldo Emerson

I thought I was alone in trying to work all this out—but everyone who has ever been alive has worked out some understanding of the world's vulnerability and his or her own. And sometimes one of them—an artist or a visionary—finds a way to express the discovery to the rest of us. My moment of epiphany, in which I understood the potential in vulnerability as never before, came to me while

I was standing in front of Michelangelo's *Pietà* in St. Peter's Basilica in Rome.

The *Pietà* is a marble statue of a very young-looking Mary holding the dead Jesus in her arms. Mary's face is inscrutably calm. Is she so accepting of her son's divinely ordained fate that she has let go of all struggle and attained a kind of peace? Or is she so overwhelmed by sorrow that her mind has disconnected to escape from the brutal fact of her son's murder?

The more I looked at her, the more I saw that Michelangelo's intention wasn't to depict either of these things; it was to show surrender. Not the surrender of quitting, of resigning from life, but the surrender to what is—to the way things happen, despite the way you want them to be. I saw the strength in surrender, the courage to understand that things are as they are. The young Michelangelo, inspired by his own genius and by the long tradition of artists before him who had painted and sculpted the sorrowful Mary, had found a way to unite utter vulnerability and utter serenity.

I had never understood this before. Though quite familiar with Catholic images, I had understood them only as part of the Catholic dogma. In that dogma, Jesus died on the cross so that he could show his followers the way to resurrection, to life eternal in heaven. But here in front of me the *Pietà* told the earthbound story: you love and you lose, and this is the way of the world. It is the way, and it is all right, if you can find the strength to surrender to it. But if you try to escape from it or get control over it—if you decide that it is not all right—you end up placing yourself outside reality, living in a self-centered delusion.

It was Michelangelo's portrait of Mary's quiet strength that gave me a new image of how to be with my vulnerability. To understand that life guarantees loss, and to surrender to that truth, was no longer a passive act of weakness or a depressing point of view. Surrender was an active decision, an act of strength and courage, with serenity as its reward. Standing in front of Mary, I saw that the way to cope with the fearful side of life was to be right in the middle of it, just as it is. I saw that I could let go of my desire to control or figure out my vulnerable human situation. I would never find an answer to vulnerability; instead, I needed to look for an answer *within* its undeniable truth.

## The Walk Around the Block

> *There are no fixtures in nature.*
> *The universe is fluid . . .*
> *There is no outside, no inclosing*
> *wall, no circumference to us.*
>
> — Ralph Waldo Emerson

I looked at Ryan, sitting across from me talking about all the ways he was fighting off vulnerability, and wondered how on earth I was going to persuade him that the first step in finding an answer to his longing was finding the courage to surrender. It wasn't a new challenge for me; in our years of teaching, Bonney and I have often joked that promoting vulnerability is just about the least sexy tack we could take. In bookstores, we survey the self-help and spirituality shelves and see title after title that promises Success! Mastery! Control! We can't promise you those, and I couldn't promise them to Ryan. But I could show him that his very own vulnerability was the conduit to a *new* feeling, one that was waiting for him, inside him, in that very moment.

I decided to tell him about a practice I call the walk around the block. It grew out of a seminar Bonney and I began teaching in New York in the 1980s called *Increasing Peace*—a kind of crash course in spiritual development aimed at helping the city's growing community of HIV/AIDS patients and their friends and families. Long before the HIV epidemic, we had come to understand that vulnerability was a key to understanding much of human behavior, but the physical, emotional, and spiritual crisis that came with the sudden onslaught of the disease—that assault of loss— threw vulnerability into our faces, and everyone's.

In the seminar, we asked people to consider their own

vulnerable situation as a bare fact of life, just as this book is asking you to do. I would stand in front of the group and ask everyone to look at me as temporary—to focus on the fact that *I* was vulnerable, that one day I would die and this body of mine they were seeing, this voice of mine they were hearing, would be gone. Then I would ask them to turn toward their seminar classmates with the same awareness. After a minute or so, I'd ask them what it felt like. One man reported that as soon as he heard my instructions, he felt like throwing up. Everyone laughed very hard at him, and he laughed, too, the laughter of nervous tension.

Then Bonney and I would take things a step further. We'd ask the students to leave the seminar room, leave the building, and go for a walk around the block, looking at every person they passed on the street with the same awareness they had just brought to their classmates. We were asking them to see everyone, including themselves, as vulnerable and temporary. This was a confrontational style of teaching, but we did it because we were working under emergency conditions. We wanted to help our students push past the blame, fear, anger, and defensiveness they felt toward life's difficult truth and see how else they could work with the reality of loss.

## Angry, Sad, in Love

> *Nothing divine dies. The beauty of nature reforms itself in the mind, and not for barren contemplation, but for new creation.*
>
> — Ralph Waldo Emerson

One bright sunny morning, a group of students in our seminar went out for a walk and came back changed.

I was waiting for them on the front steps of the building. One by one I watched them coming up the block toward me—some looking angry, some looking sad, some with tears in their eyes.

The angry ones are the easiest to describe. They found the exercise depressing and they were mad at me for ruining their morning. They had come to the seminar to feel better, and instead the contemplation of vulnerability had made them feel worse. They couldn't, or didn't want to, think any further than that.

The sad ones had had a mixed and thoughtful reaction. The exercise was upsetting for them, too, but they had also seen something new as they passed one person after another on the busy Manhattan streets. As someone young passed by, someone richly dressed, someone gorgeous, someone athletic, someone exuding confidence, the students realized that neither youth, wealth, good looks, good health, or self-esteem offered anyone anything more than the illusion of protection. The very qualities we desire most revealed themselves, in the light of this temporary life, to be empty of any enduring value.

And then there were the ones with tears in their eyes. As these students passed by the people on the street, holding the reality of our shared vulnerability in their minds, they saw through and beyond the differences among people; they saw only brothers and sisters. The social habits we're all trained in—of evaluating, comparing, judging, and distinguishing ourselves from others—had gone into suspension in these students, and a deeper level of their minds had become available to them. Each person they passed by was another living being, amazing, precious, made more so by his or her temporary citizenship in this world. Seeing this way, the students felt a brotherhood, sisterhood, personhood connection. The tears in their eyes were tears of love.

## The Mind in Oneness

> *Consciousness now finds and adores—in the sky and the nest, the soul and the void—one Energetic Love.*
>
> — Evelyn Underhill

In case you're thinking that these students did "better" than the ones who got angry—or that they *were* better, wiser, less self-involved—let me tell you about Glen, and you'll see how short the distance between them is. HIV-positive at 35, Glen was referred to me by his physician who was hoping I would be able to help him decrease his severe episodes of fear and anger. He had refused medication for his symptoms, rightly asserting that he was having extreme feelings because of the extreme situation he was in. He said he didn't want to learn any mental tricks or be hypnotized out of his feelings, but he knew he needed some new way to work with his state of mind.

I worked with Glen for a while using a meditation technique drawn from Buddhist insight meditation, and this helped him to frame his anger and fear as just two more passing experiences in the flow of thoughts and feelings constantly coming and going, coming and going, in our minds. His practice took some of the energy out of his anger, but it wasn't strong enough to get to the root of it, which was the fact that he had gotten sick in the first place. His sickness wasn't a passing thought, coming and going; it was a fact. And it was compounded by his own oppressive self-judgment. He'd always thought of people who got seriously ill as losers who'd somehow brought their illness on themselves. Now he was one of the losers, and all the more so because his illness had a social stigma attached to it.

When I asked him to join in an *Increasing Peace* seminar, hoping that the discussion of shared vulnerability would expand his perspective and soften his self-judgment, Glen posed a real challenge. At the point in my talk where I asked the group to look at me as vulnerable and temporary, and then to look at one another the same way, he stood up and started shouting at me: "Ah, give me a break! This is just some game for you. I'm the one who's fucking dying!"

He was really charged up. In such a circumstance, it is usually best to let someone have his say and discharge some of his angry energy, so I said nothing, just waited. Glen went on, saying it infuriated him that I, who appeared to be in perfect health, could compare my situation to his. He said that people like me had the luxury of worrying about vulnerability because we weren't facing it the way he had to every single day.

He was right, of course. I had faced my own death, through accident or violence, a few times—one of which I'll describe later on—but those were incidents that passed. When Glen went to bed on a Tuesday and woke up on a Wednesday, he was still HIV positive and still at risk of developing AIDS.

But he was also wrong. He was not the only one in the world staring vulnerability in the face. He had a diagnosis, I did not, but we both shared, along with everyone else, a temporary status in this world. I knew that a practice like the walk around the block had the potential to shake him out of his angry, stigmatized isolation and move him closer to connection. And on the same day he raged at me in the seminar room, Glen came back from his very first walk in tears of love.

The discovery Glen and the other students made that day was the great opportunity that vulnerability holds. Our vulnerable reality, just as it is, with no magical solutions or illusory protections, opens the door to a deeper part of our mind where boundaries dissolve and a unifying love rules. This is the mind in oneness, and we'll come back to it in the last part of this book to explore ways of cultivating this crucial part of our nature.

*What you can know for certain is that, as a created being, you are inseparably bonded to creation; you always have been and always will be. There never was a time and there never will be a time when you are not part of creation. This unbreakable bond is your oneness with all of life….*

# 6

## Practicing Vulnerability

*We sensed—we really did—this almost mystical unification of all people in the world at that moment.*

— Buzz Aldrin, astronaut, as he stood on the Moon

To teach the *Increasing Peace* seminars with fresh insights, I began to practice the walk around the block with more frequency and commitment. In just a little while, I'll talk about how you can practice it yourself, cultivating your awareness of vulnerability by turning toward other people for this crucial learning. Then we'll explore a couple of other ways to cultivate that awareness in different contexts—by looking to the natural world around you, and by looking within yourself—and see how they create the conditions and possibilities for a profound awakening.

At that time, our office was on West 11th Street in the Greenwich Village section of Manhattan. To walk three blocks in any direction was to pass scores of people of every lifestyle and nationality, as well as many cultural and religious institutions, restaurants, coffee bars, markets, boutiques, and bookstores.

I tell you this to give you a feeling for all the distractions that presented themselves to me as I tried to walk down the street with courageous eyes, looking at the people I passed with a full, clear awareness that they were temporary. Even when I left the office committed to the exercise, I would get only about 20 feet before my mind was all over the place, looking in store windows, watching people drinking coffee in cafés, wondering if I should buy bread now or later. I could explain away my distraction as a love of the vibrant neighborhood, but if I was honest with myself, I could see that my mind was happy to forget vulnerability and focus instead on the good material presence of life right in front of me.

After a block or so, I'd remember the exercise I was supposed to be doing and promise myself to do it with more willpower the next time I took a walk. I remember that promise so clearly because it was so clearly a lie: I could have simply resumed the exercise for the remainder of that particular walk. *No,* my mind was saying, *do it next time.* It was finding another excuse not to focus on vulnerability.

In my own little surrender to distraction on the street, I could see with intense clarity the seductive power of all our escapist industries—TV, movies, professional sports, drugs—that keep us busy with voyeuristic fantasies and mind games. Our minds will sign up for anything that takes our attention away from reality.

As you will see when you try the walk around the block for yourself, it is asking a lot of your mind to look at the world in this new way, even for a little while. Your mind, hardwired to ensure your survival, has been busy your whole life trying to deny the reality of your vulnerable situation. Designed to survive, the last thing your mind wants to do is to admit to your vulnerability, which implies, of course, its own.

But even though you try your best to hide from the truth of your vulnerable situation in this world, deep down your mind knows it's true. The refusal of reality is, ultimately, an impossible job—the evidence against it is everywhere. In whatever direction you turn your eyes, you are seeing living beings in front of you—plant, animal, human—that are here now but will pass away, and this includes what you see when you look in the mirror. There is no being you will ever see or meet that is exempt from this. And it's not just living things: everything that comes into existence also goes out of existence. Everything that comes to be will be gone one day. Ideas, buildings, cities, armies, religions, civilizations, all cycle on the great wheel of coming and going. It is a work of pure fiction to tell yourself that you are exempt from its turning.

## Turning to Others

> *O the joy of that vast elemental sympathy . . .*
> — Walt Whitman

To fully come to terms with this reality and the fear it engenders, you don't need to meditate in solitude for years. The people all around you can be your meditation, and the street right outside your door can be your meditation center. When you've finished reading this chapter, take your own walk around the block and find out for yourself what happens in your thoughts and feelings.

The goal of the walk is to be willing to look at everyone and everything you see as temporary. It's a good idea to prepare yourself for your walk by finding a thought or an image that helps you remember and focus on the truth of vulnerability. Without a reminder, you'll find that you quickly forget the reason for your walk and get caught up, as I did, in the ten thousand distractions of the people and the street around you. In the *Increasing Peace* seminars, Bonney and I came up with a phrase to help students stay in this awareness: we asked them to think of each person they saw as "a soul briefly here." You may come up with words of your own to focus your mind on each passing person's vulnerability. Whatever way you choose to frame it, the thought alone begins to free your mind from the impossible job of denying reality as it really is. Remembering your intention, even for only a few minutes, is enough to begin your transformation.

My own reminder is the image of Mary, because to me she represents the two sides of human vulnerability. In her form as the Madonna, the young mother adoring her infant boy in countless works of art (and on thousands of Christmas cards and calendars), Mary represents for me the entire loving energy of the world, an energy that we each experience as the desire to love and be loved, to care for and be cared for, to reproduce life and to cultivate it and watch it grow, to be creative, to have beauty in our lives, to make the world a better place, to have peace. But in her form in the Pietà, as the sorrowful mother, holding her grown son dead in her arms, Mary is the end of things— the brutal fact of loving and losing, the transitory nature of this life, the truth of vulnerability. I cannot separate the adoring Mary from the grieving Mary. When I remember her, I remember both sides of this life. There are many variations on this divine feminine representation of serenely embracing the beginning and end of life: the Mother Earth image of the Native American traditions, the Universal

Mother of Hinduism, the goddess Gaia of ancient Greece, and Buddhism's Kuan Yin. On my own meditative walks around the block, I would take the divine feminine with me as a reminder of reality.

If you live in a city, you already have a wonderful place to practice: just step out your door and start walking down the street with your thought or image in mind. If you live in a less populated area, you may need to drive to the mall or some other location where a lot of people gather. If you ever have the chance to take your walk in an airport or a major train station, you may find the experience particularly evocative in these places of transition where all kinds of people cross paths, literally coming and going, coming and going.

As you look at them with this thought, you'll expose your mind to the fact of vulnerability over and over again, and you'll start to get used to it. Eventually, it will begin to seem more tolerable. You may find it hard to look at some people in this light; for me, it's most painful to think that "a soul briefly here" describes the sweet little children who just *got* here. But I must include this point about the children, though I do so with the greatest reluctance, because it is crucial to accept that there are no exemptions from life's fragility. (I hope with every fiber of my being that I die before I see any of my children or grandchildren or nieces die, but my hope can't make a dent in that reality.)

## Meeting Your Teachers

*Could a greater miracle take place than for us*
*to look through each other's eyes for an instant?*
— Henry David Thoreau

Some people you pass will be easier to connect with than others. You'll see the vulnerability right there in plain view, etched on their faces in the form of worried and scared expressions. In these people, vulnerability broke through to the surface long ago, and now it is a permanent, perhaps unmanageable, truth in their emotional lives. They may be suffering from it full-time, except when they sleep—and even then, vulnerability may haunt them, seeping into their dreams and waking them up at 3 A.M.

Others walking past you on the street or through the mall may not seem vulnerable, but rather aloof, disconnected, or angry. Their vulnerability will be more difficult to recognize at first, but vulnerability is the very reason for those aloof or angry faces they present to the world. You can be sure that vulnerability is working on them, too, even though all you see is the defense—the mask of invulnerability they put on to convince others and perhaps to fool themselves.

Beyond the palpably worried and scared, the visibly aloof and angry, the greatest number of people you pass on your walk may appear to show no signs of vulnerability at all. They're going about their day in the ease of the present moment, as if everything is only good, with life's guarantee of change and loss the furthest thing from their minds. Your thought of vulnerability won't make any sense when you look at them. Their lives may indeed be safe and secure right now; life's basic goodness and beauty may be their current reality. But sometimes you'll get a chance to see the vulnerability rise to the surface. All it takes is a flare-up nearby—a couple arguing, a man stumbling and shouting something incomprehensible—and you see the change. A sense of threat moves through the crowd; some people tighten their jaws and narrow their eyes in an aggressive response, while others hunch their shoulders and look away in an instinctive posture of defense; the underlying vulnerability in all of us reveals itself again.

Then you may pass by a few people who have found their freedom—who have confronted vulnerability and developed a stable inner way of being, in harmony with life as life is. These are the wise ones, and it would be wonderful if we could pick them out of the crowd and ask them how they attained their wisdom. If you personally know any such people, talk with them and listen carefully to what they say.

Practicing around a lot of people is important for two reasons. The first reason is that you'll get the chance to see a whole spectrum of people—young or old, healthy or weak, handsome or homely, rich or poor, different races and different ethnicities, exuding confidence or looking scared.

By seeing them all with the eyes of vulnerability, you will realize that all distinctions among people—all the social categories that seem to separate us—are thin and ephemeral. Each person passing you will be a soul like you—another in the great human parade of courageous souls coping, as you do, with the same fact of life.

The second reason for walking in the presence of many is even more powerful. Not only do you get the chance to see all sorts of people who look different from you and realize that you're all in the same situation together; you can also let it sink in that *they* are all dealing with *their* vulnerability, each of them in his or her own way, and that deep down they share your longing for an answer to life's inevitable change and loss.

By doing so, you bridge the emotional gap that we perceive between ourselves and every other person, even our intimate partner. It is our individual, inner experience of our own intimate feelings that makes each of us feel separate and alone. But if I know that you feel the way I do, I feel closer to you, and for a while we are together in this world. In a crowd at a ball game, if we're all cheering for the same team to win, we share a fleeting sense of oneness. In a psychotherapy session, if I tell the patient that I feel the way he does, we find a moment of connection.

Now I am asking you to consider bridging that emotional gap by walking with the awareness of vulnerability amid a crowd of absolute strangers—the bigger and more diverse the crowd the better. Realizing that all of them feel as you do—that there are no exceptions to the vulnerability we all share—will start to set you free from your isolating individual fears.

## Ryan's Walk

> *The least change in the man will change his circumstances;*
> *the least enlargement of his ideas, the least mitigation of his feelings . . . And should [he] come to feel that every man was another self, with whom he might come to join—every degree of ascendancy of this feeling would cause the most striking of changes of external things.*
>
> — Ralph Waldo Emerson

Ryan and I had planned to use one of our sessions as the time for his first walk around the block. Instead, he found his own way to do it while sitting at a conference table at work.

Ryan, who was running the meeting, had seated around the table the three vice presidents who reported to him on various aspects of marketing products endorsed by star athletes. These meetings, held once a week, were dominated by his large presence and managerial pose, the same presentation of self that he had brought into my office the first time we met. Since then, he and I had grown in intimacy, and I had come to see a humbler, more vulnerable side of him, but he was surely not bringing that side to his work setting.

The walk around the block had made sense to him as an interesting experiment, but he admitted that he would probably get too caught up in his judgmental reactions to people to sense the shared vulnerability he shared with them. So he surprised himself when, on the spur of the moment, he began to look around the conference table at each of his employees with that very awareness.

In Jenna, he saw it immediately. She often made a slight movement of her lips, the beginnings of a pensive smile or perhaps a grimace, that never turned into a clear, full expression. When he'd first met her, Ryan had taken her facial gesture to mean disapproval of something he'd said, but now he saw her little expression as a way of trying to please him, to placate him. He realized that, bottom line, she was afraid of him.

Neal was an entirely different story. At the meeting, he was leaning forward over the table, facing in Ryan's direction, and as Ryan brought up the subject of dealing more effectively with one of their more difficult clients,

Neal's eyes narrowed. He looked ready to pounce, like a predator on the plains spotting prey, even though they were 28 stories up in a plush office suite.

Gary was the hardest to read. His face was expressionless, which of course *is* an expression, but whatever emotion was behind it was well hidden. Ryan saw in Gary a presentation of self that said he wasn't vulnerable at all.

They weren't sitting around that conference table discussing athletes selling sneakers as a way to fulfill their deep creative or spiritual needs. All three of them, Ryan knew, were there to make money in order to provide themselves with food, shelter, and the other necessities of life. In other words, they were all sitting there because of their survival instinct. Jenna's placating, Neal's aggression, Gary's impassivity, all were strategies to survive in the presence of Ryan.

With our discussions about the walk around the block in mind, Ryan leaned back from the conference table, fell into an uncharacteristic silence, and looked again at each of them with the eyes of vulnerability. Jenna responded with her slight smile, Neal with his body language, and Gary with a blank.

*My God,* Ryan thought, *we're all suffering.*

It wasn't a depressing thought at all. It awakened a warmth inside him and an affection toward the three of them, and with his change of mood the whole room seemed to relax. Jenna let her expression expand into a full smile. Neal sat back and put his hands, open, on the table. Gary looked curious and expectant. As Ryan broke his silence and brought up the first topic of business—a particularly obnoxious athlete client whom they had to placate—the ideas flowed, laced with humor and perspective. Rather than taking his characteristic approach of looking first for the shortcomings and negatives in his employees' suggestions, Ryan let some of their comments sink in and felt that he'd heard a batch of good answers.

Encouraged, Ryan began to practice his awareness of vulnerability more often. Inspired by the results of feeling less anxiety and more ease, he even began to conceive of writing a book on a new approach to management, one incorporating the awareness of vulnerability and reframing the workplace as a place where people could share something far richer than their survival instinct. He'd had proof, in the way he felt and in the way the work environment now felt, that awareness of vulnerability was actually a positive force. It was a great paradox for him that by approaching and accepting something so seemingly negative, he had found a path to feelings of affection and connection he'd never experienced before.

There were many times when Ryan completely forgot his awareness of vulnerability and returned to his old domineering ways. To his staff, it must have been a crazy-making experience, one moment sensing a positive change in their boss, the next dealing with his usual intimidating style. If you remember, in my own walk around the block, I couldn't sustain my intention to look around with the awareness of vulnerability even though I was the one who had developed it in the first place. This is why it is necessary to think of the walk as a practice, not just a technique to try once. As you know from other areas of your life, it is only through repeated practice that in time you stabilize a skill in you. The same is true for looking at the world with the awareness of vulnerability. It is the looking and looking again in this way that allows the mind to slowly but surely grasp our actual shared situation and to experience the freedom from fear that it brings.

So far Ryan hasn't written his book. I hope someday he will.

## Turning to Nature

> *I never lose an opportunity of urging a practical beginning, however small, for it is wonderful how often in such matters the mustard-seed germinates and roots itself.*
>
> — Florence Nightingale

A crowded street or a high-pressure conference room isn't the only place in which to practice your awareness of vulnerability. You can work to deepen that awareness—and use it to build the bridge of connection—with no one else around at all.

Many of us love to be in nature. Free for a while from the complications of other people and their needs, we can feel we are part of nature's beauty and order. A walk in the forest puts you in contact with the ceaseless creative force of life, with the orderly cycle of birth, growth, decay, death, and new birth which you can see taking place all around you in leaves and bark, bushes and buds, birds and insects, soil and water.

But to awaken this awareness in you, it doesn't take a forest; even a little garden is enough. Bonney and I had a revered teacher, psychiatrist Dr. Roberto Assagioli, who loved to retreat to the garden of his home in Florence. Naturally, we pictured this garden as some spectacular formal landscape filled with flowers and sculpture. But when we finally went to Florence and visited Assagioli's garden, we found it was a tiny strip of earth behind his house, boxed in on all sides by his neighbors' high fences. Yes, yes, our Florentine colleagues told us, Assagioli used to sit on that little patch of ground for hours looking around, joyful and content.

In any small natural space, even a tiny strip between

big-city buildings, the universal truth of change and loss is on display for you. Birth-growth-decay-death: the very turning wheel of life is available for you to consider in any patch of earth. Perhaps it's autumn with its sparseness, or winter with its bareness, where you are now, and you can't see any clear signs of nature's birth or growth. You can only see the last remnants of plants that have dried out and withered. But out of sight in the darkness of the earth, you know that there are seeds getting ready to open and give birth.

Once the birth has taken place underground, you will see the next stage of the growth process: the newborn shoots will start to rise up through the soil and break the surface of the ground. The thin green stems will thicken, leaves will begin to sprout, and then the buds will come, only to transform into flowers, which in turn transform into small green orbs. In time, the little orbs will grow larger and turn a rich red, and one day there's a beautiful ripe tomato in the summer sun. The unseen seed that started under the ground reveals its whole life purpose—to become what it was supposed to be.

Even now, at the apex of its growth process, the tomato turns a shade too ripe, and then it falls to the ground. While there may still be some buds on the plant, yet to become flowers and then tomatoes, others are lying on the soil in the early stages of decay. These rotting tomatoes still have seeds and juice inside them and their skin is still a vibrant red, but they will have no more growth.

By mid-autumn, the unpicked tomatoes that have fallen from the bush are well into the decaying process on the ground. Two months later, in the cold of winter, they will be shriveled and unrecognizable, no longer containing any juice or color or apparent life. Yet you will know that they have delivered their seeds into the soil to be born again underground.

As you sit in the garden, the mosquito that wants to bite you may live for one day, and the migrating bird that flies overhead may know life for one season. A sunny day gives way to dark clouds, and the stillness of the heat to the wind of an approaching storm. Nothing remains; everything is changing, going through stages and phases, at a visible or an imperceptible rate, and everything you witness is turning on the great wheel of coming and going, including your best ideas and your fondest plans.

When you look at nature in this way, you feel a direct connection to the world as it is, with no condition or qualification. There is nothing to think about or figure out. Nature does not ask anything of you, and it doesn't need you. It knows what to do and how to be. The seasons come and go and all their multitudinous changes happen on their own, all guided by an invisible order within—an order that guides you, too.

Beyond your name, face, body type, family history, ethnicity, status, education, and every other conceivable thing that distinguishes you from other people, the bottom line reality is that you are a created being who is part of creation. You live under the same conditions as every other created being on this planet; you are vulnerable to the same changes and subject to the same cycle of life.

Were you created by God? Are you the random product of evolution? There have been endless debates about humanity's origins, and there will continue to be. What you can know for certain is that, as a created being, you are inseparably bonded to creation; you always have been and always will be. There never was a time and there never will be a time when you are not part of creation. This unbreakable bond is your oneness with all of life, and we'll come back to it again and again as we go further on our path. It was you before you became afraid of anything in life, and it is who you still are, an identity much deeper than your fears. Just like nature, you too know what to do and how to be.

## Turning Toward Fear with Affection

> *A lost state of being is the fate of those*
> *who live undecided about the whole of life,*
> *caring only to protect themselves.*
> *They will have no hope of truly letting go*

*in their time of dying*
*because they never let go*
*in their time of living.*

— Dante

So far, I have asked you to practice your awareness of
vulnerability by looking outside yourself, at other people
or at the natural world. Now it's time to learn how to look
within—specifically, to take a close and affectionate look at
your own fear itself.

Affectionate toward your fear? That must sound like a
strange idea. The last thing any of us wants to feel is fear,
and if we must feel it, then our next best hope is for it to
go away as quickly as possible and not come back. But the
fear, and the instinct for survival that triggers it and the
vulnerability that triggers *that,* will always be part of your
experience. So, it's up to us to choose how we treat it.

You know there are times when your survival instinct
kicks in to warn you of the presence of danger. But it also
sets off alarms in you far out of proportion to any actual,
immediate threat. It does so because it is in touch with
the truth that you are vulnerable, but it cannot make fine
distinctions about what is and what isn't a real threat. Your
survival instinct isn't against you having a happy life; it's
just trying to keep you alive so that you can carry out the
purpose of your life. It isn't alarming you for no reason;
it is responding to the bare fact that your life is subject to

change and loss at any moment. Your personality has worked mightily to suppress and deny this fact, but your survival instinct has been stuck with it. While your personality has been looking out the front window at a rosy future, your survival instinct has been stuck in the back of the house seeing a flood on the way.

Turning toward your fears with affection is a way to acknowledge and appreciate your survival instinct for working overtime to protect you. When you feel anxiety, worry, or fear, you must first ask if there is an actual physical threat. If there is, you'll act on those warning signals to avoid the danger. In most situations, though, there will be no actual threat. Then you can turn to your fears and thank them affectionately for what they are trying to do for you.

My patient Catherine was a young woman almost immobilized by fear. She was afraid of entering into a romantic relationship, yet at the same time she longed to have a partner to go through life with. In general, her mind was hindered by indecisiveness, escapist fantasies, and intermittent great plans with no action. When I first advised her to try to turn with affection toward her fears, her reaction was disbelief. Her fears were ruining her life—how could she possibly like them? I asked her to try it anyway and see what the results would be.

For Catherine, worry was a particularly compelling form of fear, and the object of her worry would often be a man she was interested in. *What did he mean when he said they should stay in touch? Should she call first? How would he take it? Was he secretly addicted to drugs, like the last man she was attracted to? Would she only find out after she was too involved? How would she know?* She had a remarkable ability to recall the specificity of her worries and their lingering impact on her, and so we decided that worry would be our first test subject in her new practice of turning toward her fears with affection.

I knew we were taking on a big job. The seductiveness of worry is our belief that, by worrying about something long enough, we are going to arrive at an answer. We aren't, of course; because worry is a manifestation of our fear-based survival instinct, all it can come up with is more fear. Our survival instinct sees the world as threat, so it can only supply us with information about all the threats there are to worry about.

To help reinforce her new practice, Catherine and I used part of our sessions to sit quietly together, simply waiting for any form of fear, including worry, to come into her consciousness. It was a kind of meditating on the rising of fear.

"Oops, there's the first one," she said.

"What is it?"

She laughed. "I'm worrying about whether I'm doing the meditation right."

"Okay, good," I told her. "Now go back to the meditation and see what comes up next."

"The next one came right away. I'm worrying that I'm not doing this as well as other people and you must think I'm a loser."

I told her to turn toward the worry, thank it for trying to protect her, and to see what happened next. In the very moment that she thanked her fear, she felt her shoulders relax. Not only was the worry in her mind cut short, her body too got relief from the tension and tightness that worry produces.

When Catherine transferred her practice into her daily life, she had to do some fine-tuning. She enjoyed saving the time she'd otherwise have lost to extended worry, but she ran up against the obstacle of worrying about whether the practice itself was a good idea. She was concerned that she was no longer worrying enough and that some important things she *should* worry about were being ignored. To assuage her doubt, she decided to experiment from time to time by giving worry permission to take her down whatever road it chose.

It's an eye-opening experience when you let fear dominate your mind: think of my 3-A.M.-in-Paris mental journey. Catherine was especially prone to worry in the morning before work, so she conducted her mind experiment at the breakfast table. It didn't take long for the worry to join her there, and she allowed it to take her where it would. Her first thought was of the pile of work waiting on her desk at the office. Other worries followed in rapid succession: that she wouldn't be able to get the work finished, that she'd have to skip lunch, that she'd be in a panic by late afternoon . . .

She couldn't continue the experiment. It was making her feel sick to her stomach, and her breakfast was getting cold. And so worry, familiar to her just a few weeks before, now had an alien quality to it. She recognized it as a pattern of thoughts, but it was no longer who she was. She thanked her worry for trying to protect her, reassured herself that the work waiting for her was boring but actually simple and routine, and turned to enjoy her next sip of tea.

Of course, Catherine will continue to worry—as I will, as you will, no matter how much we may practice—but she has learned an invaluable lesson: how to recognize fear-based thinking for the limited use of her intelligence that it is. Fear starts with thoughts that seem genuinely important and things worth worrying about, but then it only generates more thoughts, feelings, and bodily sensations that support its fearful premise. This is your survival instinct talking to you, and it needs *your* help.

So whenever any form of fear arises, turn toward it with affection, thank it silently in your mind, and watch what happens. This is a quiet, simple practice; it works quite subtly; and it can change the way life feels. When your fear is treated skillfully in this way, the love of life rises naturally into your awareness. It has always been there, waiting for you to awaken more fully to it, and now you are giving it room.

*Love without conditions is love that*
*arises from the simple fact of*
*being part of creation and alive in the world....*

# 7

## Love Rises

*Live life when you have it.*
*Life is a splendid gift –*
*there is nothing small about it.*

— Florence Nightingale

The principles of the path I've taught you so far are the deliberate decision to lift denial and to open your mind to the truth of our shared vulnerable situation. By exposing your mind to a profound fact of life that we would all prefer to forget, you are beginning to normalize something that used to be a hidden cause of pain and fear.

But if normalizing vulnerability were the only result, I would not be encouraging you in this practice: you might be happier denying it for as long as you could. It is what the awareness of vulnerability leads to—what it brings out in you—that makes it a valuable practice and a step on the path to your full spiritual potential. The bridge of connection you're building and the sense of oneness you're glimpsing, whether in a crowd or alone in a garden or in the privacy of your mind, slowly awaken a new form of love in you.

I say "new" because the love that rises up in you, though it has always been part of you, has been dormant for so long you may not recognize it. The kind of love you have become used to in your life, what I'll call the conditional kind of love, has long since replaced the kind of love I mean, the love *without* conditions.

Conditional love is loving someone because of the way he or she treats you or loving a moment in nature because the sun's slant makes for an interesting light: you feel loving in response to some specific condition. Love without conditions is love that arises from the simple fact of being part of creation and alive in the world; it is the kind of love that the Islamic mystic poet Rumi meant when he described the goal of spirituality as "love without an object." In common parlance, it's simply called the love of life. This love is a force of nature, and we all have it inside us, hardwired just like our survival instinct. It is not based on any condition; it just *is*.

When this love without conditions rises, unhindered by fear, there is no more searching. When it fills your thoughts, your feelings, and your body, your questions are finished. Conflicts are reconciled, opposites collapse, separation ends. Whatever else you wanted is meaningless now. Questions, conflicts, separation, and wants only exist in a state of fear. Your unconditional love of life dissolves them.

And therein lies the key to the realistic spiritual path that we have written this book to chart. Bonney and I are teaching you a path based on the bare facts of everyone's life, without exception, that leads you right to the most essential two sides of your nature—love of life and fear of life—as your spiritual practice. Your innate love of life, with its limitless potential for connection and joy, is locked in a silent struggle with your innate fear of life, with its limitless potential for anxiety, anger, worry, and impulses of control or escape. For us, learning to respond skillfully to your fears and to utilize your vulnerability as the opening to the great love inside you is the essence of wisdom. To support this wisdom, you can add whatever philosophies, symbols, and rituals you wish; in our view, they are made significant if they serve to remind you of the elemental struggle within you and to keep you on the path to the love that you brought with you when you came into this world.

## Love on Condition

> *You are born quick to love and so will rush*
> *with love toward even the most trivial toy.*
> *This is the start of your search, your whole life,*
> *for the wrong things.*

> — Dante

How does the innate love of life in us get caught up in conditions? How does fear find its way in? Let's look at the course these two innate parts of us take to end up locked in such a struggle.

When you were small, you were wide-open emotionally. A ray of sunlight striking the wall could stop you in your tracks and have you staring at it with a smile on your face as if it was the most amazing thing in the world. Then you discovered that if you put your fingers into the ray of light, you created shadows on the wall. More amazement. But at some point something shocked you out of the light— maybe an angry voice, maybe an ungentle touch—and your openness began turning to fear that something bad was about to happen.

If you don't remember your own childhood openness, you can revisit it now, as an adult, when you look into a child's eyes. You can see the sweetness looking back at you with no protection in the way. There may be no achievement in adulthood that compares to the simple oneness with life that the little child enjoys. But there's no greater pain than watching that openness turn into a wide-open gate for fear to rush in.

Soon, you learn to close down and build defenses. You move from oneness to vigilance, watching the parent carefully to see what makes him smile or what makes her mad. You work out these necessary adaptations at a natural pace, or in haste and under pressure, depending on whether your home is safe and stable or unpredictable and violent. Eventually, you arrive at adolescence, where you will refine the defenses and solidify the patterns you've set.

At a time of great emotional turmoil, the teenage you is trying to put together some identity, some sense of self, based partly on how you feel and partly on how others react to you. You are in the wider world now: beyond the confines of your family, your peer group and the adults in your community make up your new reality. You are facing new situations and new challenges; you're being called upon to present yourself as someone who can fit into and function in the world. To do all this, you need protection.

At the same time, the teenage you is operating from an unexamined assumption that you are invulnerable and immortal. You expose yourself at times to crazy risks because you don't think for a second that something bad could actually happen to you, and your blissful ignorance of the true facts of life allows you to express the most startling confidence in your own judgments of others, especially the entire world of adults. The teenage you is a walking contradiction comprising a large child in need of protection and an immortal giant looking down on the grown-up world.

Once you leave high school, you are headed for either work or college, and in either case your contradictions have to slowly smooth out so that you can present a specific identity to others. You now have descriptions of yourself: you're someone who gets angry easily, or thinks best when he's stoned, or is hard to know, or wants to be liked, or acts aloof because she doesn't need other people. You say it is "the way I am." It is not the way you are: it's the patterns you've developed to protect and defend your basic vulnerability.

Of course, you are more than your patterns. You are still learning new things and having new experiences. Most important of all, your unconditional love of life is still in you, waiting to be aroused again. It can happen even when you feel sure it is buried forever, and it can happen in an instant.

## Love Reawakened

> *Real action is in silent moments,*
> *in a thought which revises*
> *our entire manner of life.*
> — Ralph Waldo Emerson

By the time he was six, it was obvious George was different. He didn't play the way boys usually do. His father, an alcoholic, disliked this difference and taunted George for it. George's brother joined in the taunting to gain their father's approval and keep his frightening temper from turning on him. Their mother, too, afraid of her husband's rages, began to hit George whenever she saw him do something his father would not approve.

By the fourth grade, the damage was done; George's patterns of fear and self-protection were set. George vividly remembered a moment when his teacher raised her hand to adjust her glasses and he literally jumped out of his seat, certain that he was going to be hit. The teacher looked at him as if there was something very wrong with him, which by then he was sure there was. The other students laughed at him, which humiliated him all the more.

By 13, George knew what was different about him. He was developing crushes on other boys in his seventh-grade class. He had no name for his sexuality yet, but his classmates started to call him a sissy. Between home and school, George had no refuge from violence and humiliation.

One year later, he had found an answer to his pain. Many people who become addicted remember the exact moment when they suddenly felt "normal," all right in the world, thanks to alcohol or a drug. George remembered the day he pulled a bottle of bourbon out of his father's closet and took a first, fiery sip. After that, he secretly got alcohol on a regular basis from his father's supply and, soon enough, pills from his mother's medicine cabinet.

Through the sheer power of his intelligence, even though he was stoned nearly every day, George finished high school and enrolled in a local college. To supplement his mother's medicine cabinet, his fake ID for buying alcohol, and the campus drug dealers, he began to cultivate a more dependable source: doctors. By the time he finished college, he could convince almost any doctor that he needed a prescription for anti-anxiety medication, painkillers, or sleeping pills. At one point, he had four different doctors prescribing pills and four different pharmacies filling the prescriptions.

At the age of 31, George entered a drug treatment program. He had lost his second job in a row because of heated arguments with his coworkers. The rage that is often the legacy of abused children was spilling out of him more and more, and the pills and alcohol were no longer giving him relief. The original emotional pain was long buried inside his addiction. He was desperate to change the way his life was going.

When he left the treatment program one month later, he was clean and sober, but flat broke. He had no choice: it was to go back to his family's home or to live on the street. His father had died two years earlier; his brother had married and moved far away, and he was reported to be an alcoholic, too. His mother was living in the house by herself and, despondent, George moved in with her.

He was back in the place where he had been tortured, but, like the recovering addicts we talked about in Chapter 4, he was trying to face his fear without the buffer of pills or alcohol. He sat in the basement, often in the dark, wondering how he should kill himself. He felt too ashamed and ugly to go to the Alcoholics Anonymous meetings urged on him by his counselors in the treatment program, but was too desperate not to go. Then a single quiet moment reawakened his love of life and cleared the way for him to get the help he needed. When George told me about that moment of oneness, he looked like a wide-eyed, fearless child.

It happened under the most mundane circumstances. One morning as he was taking the garbage can out to the curb, a neighbor he didn't know well passed by, walking her dog. The neighbor looked directly into George's eyes and said, "Hello." Then she kept going down the street with the dog following closely at her side. As George watched them go, the scene took on a feeling of loveliness, of rightness and sweetness. The sunlight in the trees, the companionship and ease of the woman and her dog, the early-morning noises of the neighborhood waking up and people getting ready for the day—it all sent a thrill through George's body, as though something had awakened and begun moving deep within him. He wanted to live, he wanted to get better, and he wanted to find out what life would bring.

As we go further on the path, you'll get to meet other people who have experienced the reawakening of love. You will learn about all of the wildly different conditions that aroused this love in them, and you'll get to see how the transformation of fear is always part of the experience.

# PART III

beyond fear

*Any experience in which you cross over*
*from your usual separate self*
*into a sense of connection with others*
*or with nature has some*
*taste of oneness in it, and the*
*emotion of this oneness is love.*

# 8

## The Skeleton in the Church

*If the doors of perception were cleansed,*
*everything would appear to*
*man as it is—infinite.*

— William Blake

Walking hand in hand with my little granddaughter down the path to the pond, I had no idea that an old way of seeing life was about to die away.

We got to the water's edge just as some white, orange-billed ducks, two adults followed by five fuzzy little ones, were gliding by. Curious to know if my granddaughter knew what ducks were called, I asked her, "What are they?"

She turned toward me with smiling eyes and whispered a secret just for us. "They're my friends."

A wave of sobs began to rise up in me and warm tears came to my eyes. My granddaughter glanced at me quizzically, then returned her attention to her friends. Looking at her little profile, everything bad, sad, and angry about life shattered and washed away. The pond water glistened and the ducks floated by.

We sat there a long time, wordless, watching, a 3-year-old teaching me how to see again. When the sun went behind the clouds and the day grew cool, we left the pond and walked to the local coffee bar. My little teacher got tired along the way, so I picked her up and carried her in my arms.

The coffee bar owner, a man from Bosnia whose dark, soft, worried eyes look right through you, greeted us at the door, then made my usual cappuccino and put my granddaughter's usual chocolate chip cookie on a plate. As we sat down by the window, looking out at the now gray day, I realized I was seated in paradise.

This paradise, this oneness with all of life, is yours already. You have it in you now.

Over our 40 years of listening to people's intimate stories, Bonney and I have heard many such experiences of oneness, and we've had the good fortune of having some of our own. In general, any experience in which you cross over from your usual separate self into a sense of connection with others or with nature has some taste of oneness in it, and the emotion of this oneness is love. Sometimes the taste may be brief, the love a fleeting sensation, and you are back to old you again. The moment was pleasant, interesting, desirable, but it didn't leave a lasting impression: it didn't change your idea of who you are.

But there other moments when that crossover is more complete, when the separate self with its survival instinct goes into temporary suspension and you are awakened to the love that seems to come up from the ground of your nature. Such an experience can include a host of transcendent feelings: a sense of connection with all beings; a harmonious acceptance of life just as it is; wonder at the mystery and beauty of all things; boundless compassion; utter serenity; deep gratitude for just being alive. And in such moments, free of fear, the most profound surrender to the experience leads to the most blissful state.

Words, of course, are only dimly suggestive of the experiences themselves. In such moments, you leave behind your everyday self and are ushered into a different part of your nature, where words tend not to follow. As Dante put it in *Paradise*, in such states your mind is no longer "divided," and so it doesn't describe the experience it is having: "And what became of my mind, it does not know."

But words are the only means we have to enter into other people's experiences. So for now, we'll let a few of their stories speak for themselves.

## Barbara's Vision

> *As a little flower is closed and*
> *limp from the cold night,*
> *and when the sun shines down on it,*
> *it rises to open on its stem,*
> *my wilted strength began to bloom in me,*
> *and a warm courage flowed into my heart*
> *like a soul set free.*
>
> — Dante

Do you remember Barbara, the woman we met in Chapter 3 who had lost her faith? The challenges facing her seemed to have no end.

When I first met Barbara, she'd experienced the death of her husband's sister, then her mother, and had begun to experience anxiety and intermittent shooting pains in her neck and back. In addition to several conversations about her religious journey and her lifelong search for an answer to her sensitivity to change and loss, I had shown her a meditation technique that she could use for self-care to become calmer. I had expected that our work would deepen for her, but I didn't hear anything more from here for several months. In her next phone call to me, I heard a new depth of sorrow in her voice. "You're not going to believe this—my grandson has been brought to the hospital. They think he's got cancer."

Barbara's 1-year-old grandson was admitted to the children's oncology unit with a preliminary diagnosis of leukemia. The boy's parents and Barbara and her husband camped out at the hospital, taking turns in the little one's room so that someone was always with him. On the second night, after the doctors ruled out leukemia and changed his preliminary diagnosis to a dangerously low blood platelet count of unknown cause, the tiny boy was given prednisone to swallow. Barbara was the one in the room at the time, and she watched with horror as her grandson reacted to the medicine. His eyes rolled back in his head, his whole body sagged sideways, and he began to vomit violently. Barbara instinctively grabbed him and held his shaking body while he vomited several more times on her face and neck.

The boy hadn't slept the night before, and exhausted from the vomiting, he soon fell asleep. Looking at his tiny body in the hospital crib, and at the eight-year-old girl, hairless from chemotherapy, in the next bed, Barbara went into the darkest mood she'd ever known. She went down into the sheer misery of being alive, to the certainty that this world, stripped bare and revealed for what it truly is, is a place of pain and sorrow. She gave up knowing anything, believing anything, expecting anything.

Her son and daughter-in-law, drained and exhausted by the fear of what would happen to their tiny child, were out in the hospital hallway, sleeping in chairs. Sitting next to the crib, Barbara closed her eyes to rest, too, and spontaneously a vivid image of the Virgin Mary, dressed in a blue robe and with hands extended in a gesture of welcome, appeared in her imagination.

To understand what was happening to Barbara, you need to know something about being raised Catholic. In addition to the 70 million Catholics in the United States and the 1.1 billion around the world, there are countless numbers who have left the Church. Variously described as nonpracticing, disenfranchised, inactive, alienated, lapsed, and ex-, these former Catholics can be found in Protestant churches, Buddhist meditation centers, yoga schools, and Wiccan circles—on any spiritual path, or on none. But the sacred images that are so central to Catholic piety stay with them. Trained in this use of visual associations, a disenchanted Catholic can still experience a transcendent image that rises up in her imagination and affects her deeply.

Barbara knew exactly what and whom she was seeing. All she could think was that it was a premonition that her grandson was dying. The thought jolted her, and she quickly opened her eyes.

Then she saw that her sleeping grandson had reached his little hand out through the slats of the crib and, with one finger, was very lightly touching her hand. Intense surges of energy began to radiate out of her chest, and she felt as if she were about to explode. She lost all sense of her body and her mind; she became a field of love radiating through the room. In that instant the crystalline essence of her faith, the sacred heart, had come back to her. She would tell me later it was the most important moment of her life.

The mystery of the imagination is how an image, even one with the most positive beliefs associated with it, can arouse such an intense experience of love in someone like Barbara in the middle of the worst night of her life. I suggest that it came from her very powerlessness and the depth of her surrender in that moment next to her grandson's hospital crib. She'd given up on everything—no hopes, no expectations, no control. Her survival instinct collapsed, and her innate love of life without conditions was freed to rise up and fill her. The image of Mary was the door for that profound love.

## Miriam's Meditation

> *To describe…a positive attitude that*
> *flies in the face of negative odds,*
> *Hope functions as the most*
> *genuine guide of all.*
>
> —Cathleen Fanslow

When we last saw Miriam, in Chapter 3, she had reached a low point in her life, too. Widowed for four years and having lost her father and brother in the Holocaust, she was now an alcoholic in recovery, fighting the pull of relapse as well as the sense that her "religion"—cynical, detached rationality—had failed her.

After her first outpatient counseling session with Bonney, Miriam made a promise to herself not to drink. The evenings were the toughest, when she felt the most alone, but she engaged her willpower, argued with herself each time she felt the urge, and forced herself to stay away from the collection of wine bottles in the cellar that she had failed to mention to Bonney. Three days later, at their next meeting, Bonney saw both Miriam's resolve and her struggle. Even though Miriam had rejected all talk of spirituality, Bonney decided to guide her toward a possible opening to her innate spiritual potential.

An internationally known teacher in the technique of imagery, which is the therapeutic use of the imagination, Bonney asked Miriam to close her eyes, to follow her breathing, and then, when she felt relaxed, to connect with an image of a safe place and to see it and feel it in as much detail as possible.

Bonney could see Miriam's breath slowing down, and she noticed that Miriam's eyelids were beginning to quiver. This was a sign that, underneath her closed lids, Miriam's eyes were moving in reaction to vivid images that she was seeing in her imagination, just as your eyes do when you are

having a dream. Bonney kept quiet, knowing that Miriam
was inwardly engaged in an absorbing imaginal scene.

Miriam stayed in this meditative state for several
minutes. At one point, she began to smile, and then she
let out a great sigh. When she opened her eyes, she looked
tearful and happy. She was wise enough to know that she did
not want to talk about her experience right away. Instead,
she told Bonney that she would write to her about it.

A few days later, Bonney got Miriam's letter:

> Before I left Germany as a child, I would
> walk to a lonely place in the heather when
> something was bothering me. It was a real
> wilderness with no one around.
>
> In your office, when you said "a safe
> place," my mind went back to the heather.
> I remembered the smell of the strong, good
> earthy soil, the hot sun high in the sky, the
> field of purple heather in front of me.
>
> But then I saw a big swimming pool
> with clear green water in the middle of
> nowhere. I remember a part of my mind
> saying to me, "What the hell are you
> imagining?" but I went back into the image.
>
> At the edge of the water there was a
> short, white-haired, dark-skinned man who
> said hello to me. We talked a little, and

then he invited me to swim in his pool. I told him that I'm afraid of the water. I quickly lose my breath from fear whenever I try to go into any water more than a few feet deep.

He finally persuaded me to dive in by promising to help me if I lost my breath or got panicky. For some reason, I trusted him, and I slowly lowered myself into the pool.

"Swim," he ordered me. I surprised myself by doing what he said and swimming across the pool. You need to realize that I can't swim.

"Turn and swim back—swim, swim," he said. "You can do it." I listened to him and did the exercise several times without stopping. I didn't have any trouble breathing.

Finally I got out of the water and couldn't believe it was me who had accomplished all this swimming. What kind of man was he to give me all this unexpected control and confidence? I don't know, but I believe he is my guide. I believe that he is the voice of wisdom inside me.

I opened my eyes and saw you sitting there. How did I get the courage to swim without fear? Where did this man come from? I had an immense feeling of serenity beyond any words, a happiness that I will never forget.

Miriam, too, had surrendered to her fear, and the resulting discovery of a loving force inside her gave her the courage to turn away from self-destruction and turn toward life again.

## Edina's Other Mother

*The wise silence,*
*the universal beauty,*
*to which every part and particle*
*is equally related,*
*is the tide of being which floats us*
*into the secret of nature.*

— Ralph Waldo Emerson

Born and raised in New Mexico, Edina moved away when she went to college and never lived there again. While she loved aspects of her Mexican-American heritage, she'd angrily rejected what she experienced as the guilt-producing and superstitious aspects of her family's religiosity. Edina described how her family would judge any difficulties in her young life as proof that she wasn't praying enough. She expressed embarrassment about the fact that, despite her intellectual rejection of their influence, she'd struggled for years with fears that her family might be right and that whenever bad things happened to her she was being punished for her lack of faith.

This conflict inside her resolved itself in a quietly powerful experience of oneness when she returned to New Mexico to visit her critically ill brother. While kneeling with her family in the Sanctuario de Chimayó to pray for him, she was disturbed by a sudden buildup of rage that forced her to get up and leave the sanctuary. Looking back at her family in their devotional prayer, she had to restrain herself from cursing out loud. But she also felt so vulnerable anticipating the loss of her brother that some part of her wanted to believe in the potential of their intense prayer to save him.

She left the church and walked into the bright sun of the day. Breathing in the warm springtime air, she used the charged-up feeling of rage to keep walking farther and farther away from the church and her family.

She came to a rushing brook that was high on its banks from all the melted snow flowing down from the mountains. As she stared into the churning water, she fell into a compelling vision of herself in the water, feeling it rush over her and through her, cleansing her and freeing her from the last residues of the rage. When she became aware again of herself sitting by the brook, she realized that she'd scooped up wet handfuls of clay from the brook's bank and was holding it in her hands. She looked out across the hills and felt the immense power of the earth holding her. Losing all track of time, she sat there perhaps for a second, perhaps forever.

When the oneness seemed to have faded away, she got up and began walking back to rejoin her family. Every step of the way, it felt to Edina as if Mother Earth was sending loving energy into the very nerves of her feet.

## Richard's Bliss

> *We now realize that it is the very fact of approaching spiritual awakening that causes a crisis within.*
>
> — Roberto Assagioli

I was 30 years old when the experience of surrender first happened to me. Like many people who have transcendent experiences under extreme conditions, I faced my fear in the form of a very personal taste of death.

Bonney and I, with our 9-year-old son and our 3-year-old daughter, were in a canoe crossing Lake George in upstate New York on a beautiful late August afternoon. We had started out on a narrow part of the large lake, and across the water the other shore looked to be several hundred yards away. The thick fir trees and the steep hills that encircled the lake kept us from seeing the sky except for the dome of blueness directly over our heads. So it seemed very sudden when the wind began to howl, the sunny blue sky went literally black, and booming thunder sounded very close by.

The water got choppy, our canoe began to rock, and Bonney and I got frantic, yelling at each other to turn the boat around and head back to our side of the lake. We were city people pretending to be outdoors types, but we did manage to get the canoe turned around and pointed toward our shoreline—just before the canoe flipped over. Thrown into the water, we each went for one of our kids, who were wearing life preservers. We didn't know how to do proper lifesaving, but we swam sidestroke and tugged our children along with us. By the time we got near shore where we could stand up in the water, we were both exhausted, and we used our last bit of strength to climb up onto the narrow strip of shore between the water and the woods.

Massive bolts of lightning were crashing down into the trees, and in the late-August dryness, the branches were catching fire. The forest was starting to burn, and more lightning was coming, striking both the trees and the lake. Standing there exhausted, drenched, and trapped between the lake and the woods on fire, I looked at Bonney and my kids and realized in the pit of my stomach that our time had come, that we were done, that we had just a few seconds of life left. It wasn't a fearful thought, but rather an absolute, in-the-bone knowing. Everything was over.

In those seconds before annihilation, a wave of love began to rise up in me. The love got stronger and stronger until my mind and body dissolved into it, and in the next instant the only thing left of me was bliss and the awareness of bliss. Language doesn't go with you into such a state. All I can say is that the "I" that I had lived with all my life was gone, replaced entirely by bliss, and at the same time there was an "I" that was aware of the bliss.

I don't know how long I was immersed in bliss, but the next thing I was conscious of was hearing the word "Run!"

Bonney yelled it again, and I scooped my daughter up in my arms and followed Bonney and my son in a frantic dash through the burning woods. Up ahead, I saw that she was leading us toward a large gray farmhouse she had glimpsed in one of the lightning flashes.

We got to a side door and found it open. We stumbled into a large, very dark kitchen, and we called out several times to let the people in the house know that we'd come in from the storm. There was no reply. The lightning was flashing through the kitchen window and sparks were shooting out of all the electrical sockets and light fixtures.

We slumped down against a wall away from the sparks, our drenched clothes making streams of water across the slanted kitchen floor. We called out again but heard nothing.

The bliss was still with me, though not as all-embracing, and I could see that Bonney was beginning to relax after having fiercely summoned all of her will to save her children. My bliss, though it would prove helpful in the long term in the way that it changed my consciousness and contributed to changing our lives, had been useless in the urgency of the danger in the woods. It was because of Bonney that my kids would go on to live past the ages of nine and three.

A big man in work clothes ran dripping wet into the kitchen and started talking to us as if it was perfectly fine for us to be sitting there. He said that he'd seen "balls of lightning" rolling across the fields, something he'd heard stories about but had never seen before in his forty years of farming there. Just then, from a darkened corridor off the kitchen, a tall, frail old woman carrying a small glass of sherry came into the room. "Stay as long as you need to," she said before we could even explain our presence. Then she turned and went back along the corridor. From the way she brushed her free hand along the wall to guide herself, I could tell that she was blind. The farmer followed her, and I could hear them talking about making sure to check on another neighbor.

The flashes in the window were beginning to dim, and

the sparks stopped shooting out of the sockets and lights. I got up and opened the kitchen door and saw the ground and trees soaked dark with rain. I hadn't even known that the rain had come, and in it the fire in the trees had been extinguished. Smoke was rising from the branches and the charcoal smell of burnt wood was in the air.

Outside, the storm was over and the sky was blue again. We heard the sound of a car passing by not too far away, and we climbed a muddy hill in the direction of the sound to find a road that we hoped would lead back to our campsite. The four of us, standing there drenched and shaky, must have looked like a strange group of hitchhikers waiting for the next driver that would come by.

Looking up and down the quiet road, I felt infinitely relieved and completely emptied out. I had become so insubstantial that I didn't know what I would see if I looked in a mirror. My family by the side of the road looked real enough, but I myself wasn't anything more than the awareness looking at them. I had no knowledge of who I used to be and no memory of what I used to know. I only knew for sure that I knew nothing and that, from this moment, I was starting over. Starting from zero, I had to learn something new.

Within a week, I was training in Zen. It was the start of a conscious spiritual search to find out more about the surrender and the bliss I had tasted on that lakeshore.

## Revising Death

> *O death, where is thy sting? O grave where is*
> *thy victory?*
>
> —1 Corinthians 15:55

In one form or another, each of these stories involves the nearness of death. Death is the fear of all fears, the bottom-line threat that our survival instinct struggles against all day long. But does death deserve its reputation?

In story and myth, death is often portrayed as a shadowy figure looming nearby, sometimes in a dark cloak or in the form of a walking skeleton, ready at any moment to tap us on the shoulder and take us away forever. In every time and culture, people have dreaded death, invoked supernatural forces to help them escape from it, and in some instances, such as the Psalms, pleaded with God to bring death to their enemies. Death is a subject that defies anyone to say anything good about it.

Bonney and I, though, have some things to say that may at least help you to revise your natural fear. Through our years of working in hospitals, and through experiencing the deaths of many friends and relatives, we can offer three promising facts about death for you to consider.

First, the state of being dead is not a problem. Some people speak fearfully of annihilation, of utter blackness and eternal nothingness, but you've already been there, you've already had that experience, and you got through it fine. If you envision death followed by nothingness, then you must realize that you were nothing before you were born. Do you remember any specific problems at that point? Why would you have a problem after you die? You can relax about nothingness.

Second, there is nothing difficult about the act of dying itself—everyone manages it. You didn't know how to be born, but you did it successfully, and you don't think you'll know how to die, but you'll do it, too, when the time comes. My own father, a man who to my knowledge didn't devote a minute of his life to a spiritual pursuit, looked at my mother and brothers as he lay on his deathbed and calmly asked, "Can I go now?" They said yes, and he did. He obviously knew how to do it, and you'll know how, too, no matter what the circumstances. Bonney and I tell you this with total confidence: Don't worry about it.

Third, when your time to die does come, the movement into death may turn out to be an intriguing experience. Many religions promise that after your death you'll enter into a new realm of existence; some get quite specific about the form it will take. Since these images of the afterlife can't be proven, they are acts of the imagination: either you can imagine that they are true or you can't. What we can tell you to be true is that we have seen many transitions into death that were peaceful, graceful, and reassuring.

One particular view of the dying process that has generated both great interest and great controversy comes from the near-death experience, a phenomenon reported by people undergoing surgery, heart attacks, car accidents, and other real-life moments of great physical danger. Skeptics dismiss these experiences as mere neurological events caused by opiate-like substances that flood the brain. But if they are real, they promise nothing less than release from the very fear of death and dying.

In the classic near-death experience, of which there are many subtle variations, a person who is on the verge of physical death feels himself leaving his body, going through a tunnel, and emerging into an energy field of brilliant light. In its most dramatic form, the entry into the light includes a meeting with friends and relatives who have already "passed over." Consistently, the brilliant light is said to have the quality of a loving presence that reassures the dying person and makes him feel totally safe, an amazing feat in view of the fact that he has separated from his body.

In the next stage of the experience—just a few seconds on the clock—wisdom is communicated to him, wisdom he can use if he returns to his body and resumes his life. Sometimes the wisdom takes the form of a "life review": he sees scenes from his past ("my life flashed before my eyes") in which there is an implicit teaching about how he can live better and bring more love into the world. Once the wisdom is received, the experience in the light ends, and he suddenly finds himself back on the operating table or being lifted out of the car wreck.

In his book *Reinventing Medicine,* Larry Dossey, M.D., provides a detailed analysis of the near-death experience of a fellow physician, Dr. August Reader. As the editor of the journal that published Reader's account of experiencing "wholeness and bliss" as he came close to death, Dossey was wondering, "Why should someone whose brain is deprived of blood and oxygen experience an overwhelming sense of unity with all things?" Reader himself could only offer the answer that he received from the experience itself: "The answer comes in a love that is . . . profound, deep, and unifying."

## You Too Will Be

> *Ignite the mind's spark to rise the sun in you.*
> —Florence Nightingale

Short of teetering on the brink of death, how will you come to such a moment, such a dazzling experience of connection? Your practice of facing vulnerability and turning toward fear will help you to create the conditions, but the breakthrough into love will more often than not come as a surprise.

I remember vividly the moment, on one of the art

and meditation tours that Bonney and I led in Florence, when I witnessed a woman right next to me opening to the ground of love. It was a chilly, gray day, and some of our tour members were complaining about the cold in the big church we were visiting, Santa Maria Novella. Nevertheless, Bonney and I continued our talk as we all stood in front of a masterpiece fresco of the early Renaissance, Masaccio's *The Trinity*, painted on the eastern wall.

*The Trinity* depicts the Resurrection. As Jesus on the cross is being lifted heavenward by the Holy Spirit, pictured as a white dove, and by God the Father, his mother, Mary, calmly gazes out at us, the viewer, and at her side Saint John intently watches Jesus' ascent. A little lower down, two merchants of Florence (patrons who paid for the painting) are depicted kneeling in prayer. Beneath the floor where they kneel, at the base of the fresco, there is a skeleton in a tomb with an inscription on its wall: IO FU GA QUEL CHE VOI SETE: E QUEL CHO SON VOI ACO SARETE.

When I translated the inscription, the woman traveler next to me gasped and stared at the skeleton as if it had sat up in its coffin and spoken directly to her: "I was once what you are, and what I am you too will be."

The woman seemed distressed, disoriented, looking around for a place to run to, but instead she lowered her head and began to cry softly. I got close enough to hold her up in case she felt faint, but tried not to disrupt her crying.

When she raised her head, she surprised me by looking joyful, with warm tears in her eyes. In that instant, she looked so much like the seminar students who were crying tears of love after their walk around the block.

I said nothing to her and just waited. She gave me a smile and waved me off, signaling me to leave her alone. I kept my eye on her as we walked around the cathedral a little more.

Once outside, our group settled for a rest on the steps of the church, which looks out over one of the main squares of Florence. Near the train station and a central gathering place for tourists, the square is often a parade of French, German, Spanish, Japanese, and British tour groups heading toward the church, some stopping to stare up at its magnificent facade, some going inside.

Our traveler seemed at peace as she watched the flow of people in front of us. Just to be sure, I went over and sat next to her. Before I could say a word, she gestured toward the tourists passing by. "Aren't they all so beautiful?" she said. Then she returned her gaze to the passing scene.

That evening at our hotel, I asked her about her experience in the church. She said that the skeleton's words had entered directly into her body and penetrated her mood as if she'd been injected with a powerful drug. At first she felt as if she'd "lost everything," as she put it, but the feeling was followed at once by a breakthrough of joyful energy. In hearing the skeleton's words, she felt the immediate power of a truth, and that truth set her free.

No one else in our group had a remotely similar experience. The skeleton's words had brought smirks from some of our travelers, disapproving shakes of the head from others, from still others blank stares. For some mysterious reason, at that particular moment on that day in her journey, our one traveler was ready to take in the truth of our shared vulnerable life. For each of us, it is in our own time and our own way that we allow this truth to enter and exist in us. When you do, you will know you have stepped onto the path of discovery, toward the oneness with life that you already have inside you.

*Once you've accepted, like it or
not, that you are part of life
and a full participant in its
cycle of birth and death,
you need a perspective to help you make sense of it.
I call it a spiritual perspective,
in the sense that it must
capture the spirit or essence of this world.*

# 9

## Seeking Oneness

*I see that you can't be satisfied until you are illumined by that truth beyond which there is no other truth.*

— Dante

The mysteries of vulnerability, surrender, and the rising of love in our nature certainly make this world a most curious place. It never fails to amaze me when I realize yet again that one day I simply won't be here. What a strange fact that is to take in!

If we didn't love life, leaving it ourselves or seeing those we love go out of it would be of no great concern. These events would just happen, like the sun going down at night, with nothing more to think or feel about it. I voted for this kind of detachment myself, but my sad plan to care about nothing got wrecked, fortunately, by my wife and children.

Once you've accepted, like it or not, that you are a part of life and a full participant in its cycle of birth and death, you need a perspective to help you make sense of it. I call it a spiritual perspective, in the sense that it must capture the spirit or essence of this world. When Ryan in Chapter 2 cried "Is God a sadist?" as he grappled with the way life asks us to love and lose, he was simply trying to grasp our essential situation here. Many monotheistic religions offer various perspectives on God's intentions and how to win God's favor so as to be exempted from the reality of change and loss. Other religions and philosophies have suggested that there is no single creator God, or that there is an array of gods, or that there is no higher power at all. Down through human history, people have punished and killed one another over these differing opinions: their need for an answer to vulnerability demanded that their version of reality be the absolute truth.

Our vote is with the wise people who have stepped back from the fray and reminded us that we are just tiny creatures on one very tiny planet in the infinity of time and space. If a snail could talk, I still wouldn't trust his claim to understand the forest, and our observations about cosmic truths are made from a snail's-eye view. There is a third position to take: we grow to accept that we can't know and that we have to find a way to be at home living in a permanent mystery.

And, as with any mystery worth solving, this view ensures that we'll keep searching for clues.

## The World of Seekers

> *But who am I to go? What allows me to?*
> *I'm no saint and I'm no hero.*
> *Neither I nor anyone else would think me*
> *worthy.*
>
> — Dante, on the eve of
> his spiritual journey

Bonney and I were young adults during the social and political turmoil of America in the 1960s. Assassinations, civil rights marches, antiwar protests, race riots, cities burning, college campuses shut down—and our neighbor in the apartment next door returning from Vietnam riddled with shrapnel, while other friends were being drafted or running away to Canada—these were part of everyday life.

We felt were living in a uniquely insane time, yet the most cursory reading of history reveals that it was not unique: human beings have always been reacting to one another with life-destroying fear and aggression right alongside their life-affirming developments in medicine, science, and the arts. Seven hundred years earlier, when Dante was writing *The Inferno* to describe the hell on earth that humans create for one another, he concluded that history would never change for the better until human nature itself was transformed. In our very own small way, before our career paths were clear to us, we knew we wanted to do something to help with the transformation. But we also realized that if we couldn't effect a transformation in ourselves, if we couldn't extricate ourselves from the repetitive reactions of fear and anger in our own relationships, we certainly couldn't expect anything or anyone else to change.

Once we started formal training in psychology and meditation in 1970, we began to meet many fascinating people who were seeking clues about how to live in harmony in this temporary and fragile world. It would be a joy to someday write a book describing all of them to you, but one brief conversation with a fellow seeker jumps out at me as I write this now.

He and I were sitting together having breakfast in the cafeteria of a former summer camp in the middle of Kansas that had been turned into a retreat center. The retreat was composed of a hundred people from around the country invited by Elmer Green, the biofeedback pioneer and consciousness researcher, to gather for a week and casually discuss our work.

My breakfast companion was a former Department of Defense scientist who looked like the classic science geek: thick eyeglasses, unruly hair, and four pens, each making a stain, stuck in his shirt pocket. He asked me about my work, and I mentioned that Bonney and I were exploring vulnerability as the key to understanding human behaviors.

He looked at me with a wry smile. "Ah," he said, "the second law of thermodynamics."

He had me there. "The second law of thermodynamics?"

"Everything material does only one thing."

"What's that?"

He grinned a little more. "Deteriorates."

It was early yet, the Kansas sun had just come up, and here we were talking about the end of everything.

"So, what do we do about it?" I asked.

"Ah," he said again, and said no more. We sat quietly in the mystery together and drank our coffee.

The writer, C. S. Lewis, described the mystery as a longing, as an unsatisfied desire. What happened to Lewis to evoke this longing? Quite simply, standing in the garden of his house as a child, he turned to see his brother and suddenly felt a great depth of timeless joy. He was sure that anyone who had ever felt such joy would only long to feel it again.

In framing that longing within a context of timelessness, Lewis was describing a theme of human feeling that travels down through time from generation to generation. Simultaneously, it is both intimate and unique to each person who experiences it. You can see the force of that longing in the stories of countless seekers—and in a journey that led Bonney thousands of miles across the world.

## Heading Toward Istanbul

> *All of us move across the vast*
> *ocean of being . . .*
> *each endowed with an inner*
> *knowing as our guide.*
>
> — Dante

Bonney's own longing, and her decision to act on it, illuminates the often serendipitous path that seeking takes. As you follow the various turns that made up her path, you can begin to wonder about yourself. What is calling you, what feeling is asking you to act on it?

Bonney's father's parents immigrated to America from Sicily at the beginning of the twentieth century. She never knew her paternal grandfather, but her paternal grandmother, her Nana, was a strong presence in her childhood. Nana spoke English with a heavy accent and was *analfabeta* (Italian for "illiterate"), but she was a wise and loving woman who encouraged all of her children and grandchildren to be highly educated. Only later in her life was Bonney able to truly appreciate her Nana's honest simplicity, her complete indifference to material possessions, and her deep appreciation of relationships and family.

Fifteen years after Nana died, Bonney, who by then was teaching and consulting on holistic medicine, announced that she had to go to Sicily. She didn't know exactly why, but the call was strong. In preparing for the trip, she learned that Sicily had been conquered by the Moslems in 827 C.E. When the Normans, under King Roger I, reclaimed Sicily for Christian rule in 1091, the king so valued the skill of the Islamic artisans that he used their knowledge in the construction of his cathedrals and palaces. In the Sicilian capital of Palermo, the main cathedral and the former Norman palace had calligraphic mosaics written in Latin, Arabic, and Greek.

This was fascinating to Bonney because, though she knew nothing of this history, she had been drawn to Islamic architecture, mosaic, and calligraphy ever since childhood when she had seen photos of the Blue Mosque in Istanbul. Her only other connection to that city was a college friend, Layla, who came from there. Layla had often invited Bonney to visit Istanbul on their summer breaks, but it never worked out, and they eventually lost touch.

## The Booklet

*When it comes to spiritual rejuvenation...*
*we are dealing with something very profound*
*and of fundamental importance, produced by*
*what we might describe as the linking up of*
*the personality with its intimate spirit, from*
*which a powerful flow of spiritual energy,*
*light and love is released...*

—Roberto Assagioli

In Sicily, Bonney and I drove south from Palermo across the island to the coastal town of Sciacca, her grandparents' hometown. We learned that Sciacca was a spa town whose thermal baths and vaporous caves had been a healing center for the ancient Greeks. It interested Bonney to learn this because she had been intuitively drawn to holistic healing methods many years before alternative and complementary medicine became a trend.

On our last evening in Sciacca, we went for an early dinner in a simple restaurant on the quay. We were the only ones there, and our waiter was extremely friendly and attentive. Tall, thin, and androgynous, he seemed to understand Bonney's few words of Italian, but spoke no English.

After we had finished our meal of pasta with sardines and grilled vegetables, the waiter gestured for us to stay at our table, then disappeared outside. About five minutes later, he returned with a worn travel booklet written in English. Though we had lots of travel books, we expressed our thanks, then went back to our hotel to sit on our balcony and take in the opalescent mauves, pinks, and blues of the misty sunset over the Mediterranean.

As the sky darkened and the first stars began to glimmer, Bonney went back into the room to read the waiter's tourist booklet. It focused on a church near Sciacca, the church of San Calogero.

By coincidence, we had visited the San Calogero church earlier in the day, driving the continuous switchbacks up to its setting on a promontory overlooking the town. Because of Bonney's holistic interests, we had gone to see the healing caves that were behind the church. All along the steep path to the caves was a wall with sculpted depictions of the Allied forces bombing the church and town in 1945. It was a startling sight because, the day before, we had visited the nearby ruins of the ancient city of Selinunte and learned that it too had been destroyed by a conquering army, in 409 B.C.E.

From the high vantage point of the church, we'd looked out at the small fishing boats on the sea and the busy Sciacca waterfront and tried to imagine how people had survived the bombings. Here was the church, now rebuilt, reborn, a witness to human resiliency.

As Bonney read on in the booklet, she learned that San Calogero was the patron saint of Sciacca. In the 6<sup>th</sup> century, when the population of the area was decimated by the Black Plague, he saved the townspeople by rediscovering the vaporous healing caves and waters that had been abandoned for centuries.

What she read next gave her chills. Although he was the patron saint of Sciacca, her Sicilian family's hometown, San Calogero came from Istanbul.

Her search was continuing to find its form. She knew that her next journey had to be to locate Layla and finally go to Istanbul herself.

## The Nine Planets

> *I circle around God, around*
> *the ancient tower,*
> *and I circle a thousand years long,*
> *and I still don't know: am*
> *I a falcon, a storm*
> *or a great song?*
>
> — Rainer Maria Rilke

The following September, we found ourselves boarding a Turkish Air flight.

Emerging eleven hours later through the international

arrivals door into the crowded, noisy Istanbul airport, Bonney spotted Layla immediately. Thirty-five years of separation was irrelevant—hugs, kisses, and then an exhausting blur of colors, sounds, smells, emotions, and jet lag as we made our way to Layla's car for the drive to her apartment. That first night, we just talked and filled each other in on the highlights of our lives—kids, families, jobs, memories.

Layla told us she wanted to bring us to a very special place the next day. Her friend Mehmet had invited us to observe a ceremony of the Sufi whirling dervishes at their monastery. We were surprised and delighted; we had long read and loved the poetry of Sufi mystic Mevlana Celaleddin, commonly known as Rumi, who was the founder of the Mevlevi dervishes.

The next morning, after a breakfast of olives, cheese, yogurt, cucumbers, bread and coffee, we set out with Layla to explore the city. It was a bright clear day. Workers in fishing boats docked along the shoreline of the Bosporus were grilling freshly caught fish for long lines of customers. As we walked across the long Karakoy bridge in the direction of the Beyoglu district and the monastery, tourists and locals were moving in both directions along with an amazing assortment of bikes, carts, scooters, cars and trucks zipping back and forth, while underneath the bridge, fishing boats, ferries and sailboats of every size and color were passing one another in the blue, choppy waters.

On the other side of the bridge, we followed Layla to the Tunel, a one-stop underground train that goes to the monastery's district. It was a very short ride, but in that time, in the depth of the tunnel on a crowded train with no lights in the car and only one little light at the front shining into the darkness, Bonney began to feel that she belonged here with these people. When you finally say yes to your longing, the very act of seeking brings you joy.

Once off the train, looking for the monastery entrance, we wandered in and out of small streets filled with shops where people were making and selling zithers, ouds, baglamas, and other stringed instruments similar to lutes. We noticed a group of what looked like American college students gathered at an iron gate with a small building on the other side. They, in fact, turned out to be German college students wearing baggy pants and soccer T-shirts and carrying big knapsacks. When they heard us speaking English, one of them came over and asked, "Please—what hour open?" We noticed that he was holding a German translation of one of Rumi's books, and we realized that we'd found the monastery.

Eventually, Mehmet showed up to meet us, a tall, lanky man, carrying a guitar in a cloth case strapped to his back. Speaking perfect English, he said that today was Rumi's birthday and for this occasion the dervishes were letting some observers in, including people from the media.

The gates were opened for all of us, but there was still a half hour wait before the ceremony (*sema*) started. We wandered around the garden, and Bonney noticed a tree heavy with red pomegranates, fully ripe. She smiled, remembering all of the pottery ornamented with pomegranates in Sicily and how her visit there had set this journey in motion.

When the doors to the monastery opened, we entered a small octagonal hall of dark brown wood with three rows of chairs around the edge of a polished floor. Layla, Mehmet, Bonney, and I all chose front-row seats. Overhead, on a small balcony, three musicians were softly tuning their instruments—an oud, a flute, and a frame drum.

The peaceful atmosphere was suddenly broken by a rush of media people with cameras, lights, and notebooks pushing through the small front entrance to get a good spot for the *sema*. There must have been twenty of them, and from across the room we could hear them speaking a variety of languages. The impatience and noise and nervous energy that they brought into the hall looked as if it was going to ruin the *sema*. Shoving for a good position for their cameras, they were actually blocking the entrance of the dervishes and their path to the wooden floor.

But as the media people slowly became aware of the dervishes behind them, they stepped to one side or the other, parting in the middle to let the men pass. A row of ten dervishes in tall brown hats and brown robes came through the gap, bringing with them a quality of concentration and determination.

The three musicians in the balcony began a slow, reflective song. Nine of the dervishes took off their brown robes, revealing their meditation clothing of white robes tied with sashes at the waist, and formed a circle around the dance floor. Each of them then walked up to the tenth dervish, who was the leader or *sheikh,* receiving a gesture of encouragement from him that gave them permission to move onto the wooden floor and begin to whirl.

At first, the nine dervishes whirled in a circle, but then they slowly moved off to establish their own space, their own axis. The tenth dervish wove in and out of their whirling, imperceptibly signaling to them, and they responded by subtly adjusting their posture or movement. Mehmet explained to us afterward that part of the leader's role was to make sure the dervishes had their heads tilted in just the right way so that the whirling didn't make them dizzy.

Bonney sat as close as possible to the dervishes, and she could smell their sweat and see the expressions on their faces as each passed by us in his circling of the floor. She could feel the air being brushed across her face like a warm breath as the dervishes' heavy robes spun round and round. There were only two sounds—the rhythmic drone of the music and the whoosh of the robes.

As the whirling intensified, she wondered if they were

in a trance. How long could they do this? They seemed to have become weightless, their outstretched arms looking like wings lifting them upward, yet still anchored by their feet touching the ground. Bonney also felt a sense of anxiety watching them. Was it safe to do this? What was it like to surrender to such a practice, such a feeling?

The media people were absolutely still—no cameras going, no lights on, no notebooks out. As the circling began to slow down, the music slowed, too, and the dervishes finished their dance by folding their arms across their chests, bowing their heads and withdrawing to the edge of the floor.

One dervish was standing right next to Bonney, and she studied his face intently. His eyes were closed, his expression serene and inwardly absorbed. Bonney closed her eyes, too, to try to feel the dervish's presence. She didn't know how much time had passed, but the next thing she felt was a palpable sense that the dervish had moved away from her.

The dervishes were resuming their positions on the floor and beginning to whirl in place again. In that moment, Bonney felt a release from some deep fear. Something in the dervishes' abandon had inspired her own capacity to surrender, and the rest of the *sema* was an escalation of joy. With the dervishes whirling in place faster and faster and beginning to circle the floor again, Bonney felt at one with them, with the drone of the music, the whooshing of the robes, the guidance of the *sheikh*. She was finally, fully, at home in the world, unaware of time, unaware of any separation between herself and others, a loving witness to the wonder of what she was seeing.

It sent chills up her spine a few minutes later when the ceremony ended and the *sheikh* stepped forward to say, in Turkish and then in English, that the most important teachings of Rumi had to do with the release of separation. This, he explained, was because at the deepest level we are one.

*You now know it is possible to turn
toward your fears without fear.
And you now know that your natural
instinct for survival is balanced
by your natural capacity for oneness.*

# 10

## The Ground of Being

*We might refine the Golden Rule as follows:*
*"Do good unto others because they* are *you."*
— Larry Dossey, M.D.

In his darkest hours, locked up in solitary confinement by the Fascist police in Rome at the start of World War II, my teacher Roberto Assagioli transcended fear, rage, and self-pity by recalling moments of oneness he had experienced and using them as a focus of meditation. No enforced isolation could shut him away from the wonder he had discovered in those moments: "a sense of boundlessness, of no separation from all that is, a merging with the whole."

Assagioli used the word *transpersonal* to describe such states; so did another pioneering therapist of the early twentieth century, Swiss psychiatrist Carl Jung. Transpersonal means "beyond the personality," and Assagioli and Jung felt, as scientists of human nature, that such transpersonal experiences were worthy of close study because they produced observable, beneficial changes in people's mental outlook, emotional balance, physical calm, and spiritual knowledge. Clearly, if a pill could give us this, it would sell in the billions. The fact that something dormant in our own nature can rise up and give us this is wondrous.

Assagioli and Jung met with skepticism from their scientific colleagues because there was no way to prove objectively the cause-effect aspect of such experiences: in my bliss experience, for example, there would be no way to "prove" that my surrender to imminent death opened me to bliss. It could be argued that bliss happened to me, for whatever reason, on that occasion only, and that my next encounter, or someone else's next encounter with imminent death, might be entirely different. There is no way to definitively predict that the nearness of death and the arrival of bliss are connected, even though there are numerous testimonials to that coinciding event, including some of the stories I've shared in Chapter 8. When my father asked on his deathbed, "Can I go now?" and then died, a certain smile crossed his lips that my mother and brothers had not seen in his lifetime.

Another common challenge to transpersonal experiences of oneness is that they do not reflect another dimension of reality but instead are just powerful fantasies. Controversy about the near-death experience has particularly focused on this distinction. The argument goes that people do not really cross over into another dimension and meet their dead relatives; rather, their meeting "on the other side" is a wished-for fantasy in their minds and, under the pressure of sensing they are about to die, their fantasy rushes into their mind to soothe them. Leaving aside the fact that there are several relatives I do not want to meet again, what is the conclusion a rational person can reach about such stories?

## Proof

> *Mankind must make heaven before we can "go to heaven" (as the phrase is), in this world as in any other.*
>
> — Florence Nightingale

Bonney and I have followed the debates questioning the factual reality of transpersonal experiences for many years, and we have borrowed our own conclusion about these experiences from Assagioli, who pragmatically decided that since such experiences are positive and life-affirming, they're real enough for him. He cites as one example the skeptical claim that the illuminating visions of St. Francis of Assisi were actually produced by an epileptic condition. If so, Assagioli reasons, the widespread impact of St. Francis's inspired teachings on wisdom and compassion should certainly make us rethink aspects of epilepsy. If a woman comes back from a near-death experience convinced that in the brilliant light she met dead relatives, and now she no longer fears death herself, has a renewed sense of life purpose, and behaves with increased kindness toward everyone . . . where's the problem?

But the pragmatic conclusion is not just our own personal preference. Much of the modern medicine you accept from your doctor is based on exactly the same pragmatism. We don't know why many medicines work the way they do, but if they work, we use them. Aspirin has long been commonly and effectively used to reduce headaches, pain, and fever and to thin our blood to lessen the chance of heart attacks, and yet for many, many years we had no idea how the substances that make up aspirin caused these benefits to happen. Would you have refused to take aspirin until you were provided with definitive proof of how it worked? On a grander scale, a force in the universe that we call electromagnetic energy is what gives you light when you switch on your lamp, and it's unlikely that you've sat around questioning its reality.

We rely on pragmatic conclusions for so many mysterious processes in our world, and transpersonal experiences may for now need to be among those on the mystery list, even though as I write this the situation may be changing. In the Epilogue, I'll cite how some of the scientific advances in the ability to photograph the activities of the brain are now providing objective evidence of the factual existence of a dormant state of oneness deep in your nature.

In his classic book, *The Varieties of Religious Experience*, William James, the father of American psychology, wanted to bring together his own conclusions about such surprising moments:

"Our normal waking consciousness is but one special type of consciousness, whilst all about it . . . there lie potential forms of consciousness entirely different."

He saw that these "potential forms of consciousness," which he had personally experienced, ". . . converged towards a kind of . . . reconciliation. It is as if the opposites of the world, whose contradictoriness and conflict make all of our difficulties and troubles, were melted into unity."

## Your Personal Challenge

*I am so small I can hardly be seen.*
*How can this great love be inside me?*

— Rumi

As you think back over the experiences I've described in Part Three, you see that they do indeed take us beyond the personality, outside our normal understanding of who we are. In each of the stories, someone is liberated from the narrow confines of the sense of self we normally live with; he or she tastes an expansion, an opening, a connection and unity with all of life. These moments of release from the "inner prison," as Assagioli called our self-conscious separateness, become powerful memories that last long after the momentary experience fades and separateness returns. The memory of oneness is part of the person's identity now, and it can do great good there. This is the kind of memory that sustained my teacher in his ordeal—the kind that moved him to write, after one such experience, "Joy is the very substance of reality itself."

But you can use this information to its fullest only if you challenge yourself to decide what you really think and believe about these stories. They happened as written to a wide variety of people—that's objectively true—but what do you truly make of them? I know that I asked you to start out on this realistic path with a very unappealing practice—to lift the veil of denial from your deepest source of fears and vulnerability—but it was always in the service of getting here, to the discovery of the oneness. And you don't have to go to Bonney's Istanbul or Edina's New Mexico hills or have Ryan's midlife crisis or Barbara's suffering to make this discovery for yourself. What you have to do is decide whether or not there is something of fundamental importance at the core of reality, in the ground of your being, and whether the direct experiences of these people point the way.

I emphasize this challenge now because Bonney and I have heard many transpersonal stories over the years from our colleagues and patients and meditation students with a missing link: they had not yet given the experience a clear meaning for themselves. Though they told us their stories in slightly hushed tones, letting us know they were sharing an intimacy, a secret even, that they had carried inside for a long time, they were still referring to the experiences as "weird" or "strange." We heard such dismissive descriptions often enough that we ended up retorting, "You're not allowed to say 'weird'."

It was said lightly but meant seriously. It was meant to challenge them to penetrate further into what the experiences said to them about the potentials in their nature. It was meant to convey what this journey we've taken together in this book was meant to communicate— that you can taste a greater reality that transcends the natural, factual fear in this life. Sometimes the experiences come as the result of surrender to dying, as in my case on the lake; sometimes in terrible adversity, such as George's years of humiliation and addiction or Assagioli in jail; sometimes in the art on a church wall in Florence; sometimes in deliberately changing one's consciousness, as Miriam did in her guided meditation and Ryan did in the conference room. However and whenever the experiences come, and however mild or intense they are, the moments of oneness leave a trace, and we know we will never be the same.

Wisdom, fearlessness, and boundless connection break through into our habitual lives like a great light suddenly shining into the dark. We are illuminated by a fresh new way to feel and to see life. The light wakes us up from living our lives half asleep, sometimes for years, sometimes for our whole existence. Those moments when the light wakes us up are never forgotten. When Miriam said that her happiness was unforgettable, she was registering the full impact of the light shining through her years of grief and emptiness.

The impact of oneness tells us something vitally important. Underneath our fear is a reservoir of love so vast that even a momentary taste of its depth can change a life. The bliss changed mine, motivating me to train more deeply in meditation and psychospiritual development and led me to teaching and traveling and writing and meeting so many interesting people. But most of all, it led me to the knowledge that, beyond all the change and loss in life, the ground of being is love.

## Life as Life Is

> *The essence . . . is summed up in these two*
> *experiences— union with the flux of life and*
> *union with the Whole—and these experiences*
> *are well within your reach.*
>
> — Evelyn Underhill

You now know it is possible to turn toward your fears without fear. And you now know that your natural instinct for survival is balanced by your natural capacity for oneness. Your innate qualities of wisdom, connection, courage, and bliss offer you a way to a better life, a life fully lived.

I find it intriguing that facing and accepting something as fearful and sad as the temporary nature of our time here on earth can lead us to a breakthrough into our ultimate state of fearless joy. It tells me that attempts to control our fears or escape from them are missing the point of how to live: the bare truth of life defeats both easily. Instead, there is a way to be with life as life is—and when you find it, something deeper in you rises up after waiting so long for you to awaken it.

Oneness arising makes me a believer in the goodness inherent in our nature and in the world. How else could it be that when we fully and willingly engage with life's worst guarantee, we are moved to smile with serenity?

It makes me think again of standing in front of

Michelangelo's Mary. We start by knowing her as the young adoring mother gazing at her infant son; we end by seeing her 33 years later as the grieving mother looking at her grown son dead in her arms. She smiles serenely at first and serenely at the last. In the face of the truth of life, her eyes don't look away, never turn away, no matter what.

# Epilogue

## *Mind and Soul*

*The desire to live life to its fullest,*
*to acquire more knowledge,*
*to abandon the economic treadmill,*
*are all typical reactions to…*
*experiences in altered states of*
*consciousness…fear of death*
*is typically quelled…the deep*
*internal feeling of eternity is*
*quite profound and unshakable.*

— Edgar Mitchell, Apollo astronaut

In the past, states of oneness and bliss were considered the property of religion and the province of mystics. But we are living in a time when it is the scientifically minded seeker, not the religious believer, who is making the breakthrough discoveries about the mystery we all participate in. In

Western culture, models of the cosmos as the territory of a rewarding and punishing creator are giving way to a vision of dynamic energies interacting at every level, from macro to micro: out there in an infinite universe and here within our tiny individual selves.

The popular image of the scientist is that of the preeminent rationalist, even skeptic, interested only in objective, quantifiable facts. But in truth, the scientific method originates in mystery: it developed in the 16th century as an alternative to religion, a new way for people to fathom the unfathomable. Before it emerged, university education had been reserved for the aristocracy and the clergy; the purpose of the university was to study philosophy and theology, and the method of study was rhetoric and discourse, not factual inquiry. Seekers such as Thomas Aquinas risked persecution when they broadened their search for truth to include the objective examination of nature, of things as they were.

One modern seeker who bridged science and religion was Wilder Penfield, a Canadian neurosurgeon who pioneered consciousness research in the mid-20th century. His lifelong search was to understand the nature of consciousness as it arose in the physical organ of the brain; he wanted to know if neuro-electric and chemical reactions could explain the human mind. As it turned out, he found no definitive answers, but he believed that one day the mystery would be solved. "In that day of understanding," he wrote, "I predict that true prophets will rejoice, for they will discover in the scientist a long-awaited ally in the search for Truth."

By chance, years after Penfield's death, Bonney and I attended a conference in Toronto and met a nurse who had assisted him in his research. She told us that Penfield had been one of her father's best friends and that he'd had dinner at their house many times. Then she leaned forward conspiratorially and whispered to us, "Wilder was looking for the soul."

## A Picture of Oneness

> *So, what is being offered to you is not merely a choice amongst new states of consciousness, new emotional experiences...but, above all else, a larger and intenser life,,,a total consecration to the interests of the Real.*

— Evelyn Underhill

Today, we can look in ways yesterday's seekers did not dream of. Using SPECT (Single Photon Emission Computed Tomography), we can photograph the brain in different states—you might say we can photograph the states themselves, yielding a picture of pain or a picture of love.

SPECT imaging visually documents the dramatic

differences between your brain in a state of fear and your brain in a state of meditation. If you are worrying, for example, certain areas of your brain become electrically excited, while other areas grow dim; both can be photographed. If you begin meditating—and keep photographing along the way—you'll see the area of your brain excited by worry begin to quiet down and new areas awaken.

Much of this research has been done with the help of advanced meditators who are able to voluntarily quiet certain areas of their brains and awaken others. It's quite a feat for these meditators to enter peaceful states of awareness under laboratory conditions; you might feel discouraged wondering how you, without years of meditation training, could begin to take advantage of this new understanding of the brain and generate more peace and equanimity in your *own* brain. You should not be discouraged, though—just the opposite. The meditators aren't doing anything you couldn't do; they are entering into brain states that exist in all of us, dormant, and simply waking them up.

One leading researcher, Andrew Newberg, while at the University of Pennsylvania, discovered a specific, important brain state of this kind, which he called "absolute unitary being" (AUB). In the state of AUB, our self-conscious sense of ourselves as separate beings drops away and in its place we feel and see only connection with all things.

Does this sound familiar?

Newberg had found a way to photograph oneness—to capture, what has been described as "moments of elevated experience" when we step outside our boundaries and "overflow with love." He hypothesized that this state of AUB may actually be the condition that different religions call heaven, nirvana, or paradise—by any name, the ultimate experience of human life.

Earlier in this book, we talked about the need for "something more," the undefinable quality of meaning and connection that we long for when the truth of the human condition hits us and we haven't yet transformed our fear. The existence of AUB suggests that when people say they know there is more to life, they're absolutely right—and we may soon be able to define the undefinable and to experience what that "more" truly is.

# Acknowledgements

We have filled this book with quotations because they remind us of the ceaseless longing and searching of people from so many times and cultures to find the way to be in harmony with life as life is. Humanity has experienced suffering from many sources yet there have always been people who in small and grand ways have found resilience and skills to survive and grow. Realizing this fact of our common vulnerability is actually an aspect of *oneness* that offers hope in the possibility of moving forward. We are not alone.

We appreciate being granted permission by Indiana University Press to use selected quotes from Mark Musa's superb translation of Dante's (Florence, Italy, 1265-1321) *Divine Comedy.* This work then inspired us to create and produce *The Florentine Promise: A Seekers Guide* in which we modernized the spiritual journey so eloquently described by Dante. Blending images of Florence, Dante's insights and our commentary, the book offers contemplations on the spiritual journey.

Our quotes from Rilke's (Austrian, 1875-1926) *Book of Hours* were translated and adapted by us. Richard Grossman's guiding comments in his two books, *A Year with Emerson* and *The Tao of Emerson,* renewed our appreciation of the beauty and wisdom Emerson's (American, 1803-1882) words.

We also drew from the genius of Emerson's contemporary, Walt Whitman (American, 1819-1892), author of *Leaves of Grass*, who was born in our current hometown of Huntington, New York. Whitman's brother served as a soldier in the Civil War. He went south to find and care for his wounded brother. He practiced nursing at the hospital in Washington. Whitman wrote extensively, as a journalist and a poet, about the brutality and suffering he witnessed and its effect on him.

We've taken words of wisdom and compassion from Florence Nightingale (English, 1820-1920). Nightingale was the creator the modern profession of nursing. She was a brilliant and fearless pioneer in bringing healthcare to the soldiers in the battlefields of the Crimean War. This was at a time when the overwhelming cause of military death was from starvation, infection and no place of shelter. As a child, she was always drawn to learning and caring at a time when nursing didn't exist as a profession in Victorian Britain. Nightingale was from a family of influence and affluence where females weren't supposed to work and were groomed to become proper housewives. She persisted in becoming educated and creating a role of nurse that she practiced. She spoke of nursing as her "must." It was her soul's calling. We learned about the great scope of Nightingale's life and practice through Barbara Montgomery Dossey's excellent book, *Florence Nightingale: Mystic, Visionary, Healer.*

We greatly appreciate permission from Cathleen Fanslow, a contemporary visionary nurse, to integrate quotes from her book, *Using the Power of Hope to Cope with Dying.* Cathleen is a pioneer in envisioning the creation of care for patients at end of life and a leader in hospice care nursing. Bonney was fortunate, when working the night shift in her first nursing position, to have Cathy as her first supervisor. She is a treasured resource for understanding the important fact that connecting with hope is always possible.

Another visionary, Larry Dossey, has been a pioneer in bringing intelligent spirituality and the transpersonal view of human nature into healthcare. His work has inspired us for many years, and we thank him for permission to use quotes from his books, including his first breakthrough work, *Space, Time and Medicine.*

We also thank Marilyn Barry for her generous permission to quote from her excellent translation of Roberto Assagioli's *Transpersonal Development: The Dimension Beyond Psychosynthesis.* The right translation always includes the benefit that the translator has truly grasped the original author's meaning, and Marilyn has fully accomplished that.

We also have gratitude for the many health professionals who have studied Clinical Meditation and Imagery with us and have shared their intimate stories and experiences.

Perhaps most of all, we acknowledge the privilege of working with hundreds of patients and clients and being brought into the intimacy of their lives.

# About the Authors

Richard Schaub, Ph.D., and Bonney Gulino Schaub, R.N., M.S., are committed to bringing the objective reality of higher states of consciousness into reducing human suffering. Seekers, clergy of every faith, doctors, nurses, therapists, lawyers, people in recovery, people challenged by chronic illness, artists, writers, and others who must draw upon their creativity and inner strength daily have sought out the work of Richard and Bonney for so many years.

Co-founders of the Huntington Meditation and Imagery Center (1980) and on the faculty of the Italian Society for Psychosynthesis Therapy in Florence, Richard and Bonney are the authors of *Transpersonal Development: Cultivating the Human Resources of Peace, Wisdom, Purpose and Oneness; The Florentine Promise: A Seeker's Guide; The End of Fear: A Spiritual Path for Realists; Dante's Path: Vulnerability and the Spiritual Journey; Healing Addictions: The Vulnerability Model of Recovery.* They have taught internationally to professional and self-development audiences in Canada,

Germany, Sweden, Holland, Italy and throughout the United States.

Prior to private practice in New York City and Huntington, Long Island, Richard's past work includes cardiac and cancer rehabilitation, counseling in an alcohol treatment center, directing a hospital-based program for adolescents, and teaching in graduate school at Hofstra and St. John's University.

Prior to private practice in New York City and Huntington, Bonney worked in medical-surgical and in-patient psychiatric and community-based substance misuse treatment settings. As a pioneer in holistic nursing, she taught at the College of New Rochelle's pioneering master's program in Holistic Nursing. She has contributed two chapters for each of the past 7 editions of *Holistic Nursing: A Handbook for Practice.*

Bonney and Richard brought innovative mind-body-spirit principles and services to New Yorkers at the height of the first AIDS crisis and also the World Trade Center attack. In this current time of pandemic, they have been working extensively with nurses and others who have been bearing witness to the profound suffering and loss of both patients, colleagues, friends and family members.

In addition to four years of postgraduate training and certification in the transpersonal psychology of psychosynthesis, they have studied brain-wave biofeedback at the Menninger Foundation lab of Elmer Green, trained extensively in Zen and in mindfulness, studied Qi Gong with Dr. Ching Tse Lee, and traveled extensively to deepen their understanding of the emotional healing principles in various spiritual traditions. Their studies led them to the monastery of the medieval mystic Hildegard of Bingen in Germany, and to the Sufi Rumi's Mevlevi order in Istanbul; they have also guided others on sacred art and meditation retreats to Florence. They now bring this synthesis of professional and personal study to their Clinical Meditation and Imagery (CMI) training to health professionals internationally.

# Artist's Statement

*I have had a lifelong appreciation and love for photography. I am drawn to film photography because of the color and quality it allows and how personal the process feels. My work is constantly changing, but this project revealed thematic consistencies, such as a calming relationship with one's surroundings and an appreciation of nature. I seek to capture the healing connection to my environment and the type of isolation that cultivates positive introspection. My wish for this selection of work is to be beautiful but only in a way that feels real.*

*I first fell in love with taking photographs while exploring my hometown on walks alone. Most of these images came from times with myself or loved ones, appreciating the beauty of my surroundings and the people around me. It is essential to find beauty and gratitude in one's environment to feel truly peaceful, or at least that is what I think. After spending time in places dear to my heart, I feel encouraged to create. Nature inspires new work and cultivates a stronger connection between myself and my environment. Spending time alone is accessible and*

*incredibly enlightening, something anyone can do, anywhere.*
*Nature is always there to encourage growth and healing, as it*
*does best.*

Ava Grace Brosnan

# Suggestions for further reading

*Mysticism: The Nature and Development of Spiritual Consciousness*
Author – Evelyn Underhill (1875 – 1941)

*The Tao of Emerson: The Wisdom of the Tao Te Ching as Found in the Words of Ralph Waldo Emerson* (2007)
Emerson (1803-1882)
Edited with an introduction by Richard Grossman

*Leaves of Grass*
Walt Whitman (1819-1892)

*Transpersonal Development: The Dimension Beyond Psychosynthesis*
Roberto Assagioli, MD (1888-1974) Translation by *Inner Way Productions* (2007)

*The Divine Comedy*
Dante Alighieri (1265-1321)
Translation by Mark Musa

*The Florentine Promise: A Seeker's Guide (2014)*
Richard Schaub, PhD and Bonney Gulino Schaub RN, MS

*One Mind: How Our Individual Mind Is Part of a Greater Consciousness and Why It Matters (2014)*
Larry Dossey, MD

*Florence Nightingale: Mystic, Visionary, Healer* (2000)
Florence Nightingale (1820-1910)
Barbara Montgomery Dossey

*Using the Power of Hope to Cope With Dying: The Four Stages of Hope* (2012)
Cathleen Fanslow

Printed in the United States
by Baker & Taylor Publisher Services